ART

IN EAST AND WEST

ART
IN EAST AND WEST

An Introduction through Comparisons

Benjamin Rowland, Jr.

1 9 5 4

HARVARD UNIVERSITY PRESS · CAMBRIDGE

PREFACE

The comparison of works of art widely separated in time and place invariably opens new possibilities of interpretation. The examples illuminate one another, mutually revealing hidden facets of their respective cultures.

The present book is a collection of such comparisons, representing the Oriental and Occidental points of view. These are not designed to illustrate the influence of one culture upon the other. Nor is this the kind of picture-book in which works of modern art are placed next to examples of primitive painting or carving in order to confer validity on contemporary artists by endowing them with the authority of tradition. Neither is it the familiar collection of illustrations of objects of different periods and places, in which the reader is invited to draw his own conclusions from these often striking similarities.

The comparisons presented here illustrate accidental parallels in the art of the East and West, stemming from a common background or affected by similar circumstances, social, artistic, and technical, in the process of their making. The subjects have been arranged in categories of figures, portraits, religious images, landscapes, birds, beasts, and flowers, and still life. These works of art have been analyzed in considerable detail both from the technical and aesthetic viewpoints in relation to their historical background, and possible conclusions have been suggested on the basis of these analyses.

A study of these pairs is intended to point out the aesthetic properties peculiar to the Eastern and Western points of view toward art and to show how parallel artistic climates inevitably produce a peculiar kind of expression appropriate to its moment and place in art history. Relatively few of the subjects chosen are contemporary with each other, for the reason that the conditions behind their creation did not happen to coincide chronologically in the history of the East and West.

The notes in this book have been arranged in order to enable the student and lover of art to share in the pleasure of discovery. It is hoped that they will have a fuller understanding of the less familiar objects of Eastern art, and will be able to enjoy through a new approach, old friends in the Western tradition. These selected comparisons are intended to demonstrate the entire artistic validity of each monument discussed, not only for the moment and place of its creation, but for all time, as an illustration of the endless variety and renewal of the creative process in operation.

This book could not have been written without the coöperation of many friends in different fields. Unfortunately it is impossible to mention all who have assisted in this complicated task. I am especially indebted to Professor Jakob Rosenberg of Harvard University for his reading of the text and many helpful suggestions. For a painstaking revision of the style of the book I must thank Miss Mignon Couser, and Miss Andrée Luce for her assistance in proofreading and preparation of the manuscript. I owe a final debt of gratitude to my wife for her continued supervision of the writing, the preparation of the text, and, above all, her encouragement to bring the work to completion.

B. R., Jr.

Cambridge, Massachusetts
July 1, 1954

CONTENTS

LIST OF ILLUSTRATIONS

INTRODUCTION

Art in both the East and West can be divided into traditional and nontraditional types of expression. A traditional art is the creative expression of a society, in which every form of creation—painting, sculpture, architecture, and even the slightest articles of everyday use—is fashioned not only for its utility, but as an appropriate symbolical revelation of those supernatural powers that are believed to govern the terrestrial order.

As the famous scholar of ancient Mesopotamian art, Walter Andrae, said,

In order to bring the invisible realm of the spiritual and the Divine within the range of perception, humanity is driven to . . . embody in a tangible or otherwise perceptible form, to materialize, let us say, what is intangible and imperceptible. It makes symbols, written characters, and cult images in earthly substance, and sees in them and through them the spiritual and Divine substance that has no likeness and could not otherwise be seen.[1]

Such an art could be called magic, since its purpose is either to give man control over the great powers that he represents in symbol or to enable him to apprehend the infinite, as displayed in a tangible icon or diagram. Its efficacy depends not upon realism of definition, but upon the representation of what the artist and his fellows in a traditional society recognize as the essence of the thing portrayed. A traditional art could be described as a functional one, since in it religious images, as well as tools, are made for efficiency. They are made to work, and they can only perform their separate functions, magical and practical, if the artist has properly followed the rules of his craft and the various prescriptions and taboos calculated to produce a magic effigy of an unseen power. It is this combination of spiritual and mechanical functions upon which Horatio Greenough spoke so well in his description of a native war club.[2] Part of the efficiency as well as the beauty of such objects will depend upon the rightness of their making, from the point of view, not only of material and technique, but of the laws respecting proportions and measurements that generations of craftsmen under priestly supervision have developed as appropriate to the end.

[1] *Die Ionische Säule, Bauform oder Symbol* (Berlin: Verlag für Kunstwissenschaft, 1923), p. 65.

[2] *Form and Function, Remarks on Art by Horatio Greenough*, ed. Harold A. Small (Berkeley: University of California Press, 1947), p. 59.

The simplest form of this magic art is found in primitive man's representation of beasts, with the idea of obtaining power over his quarry in the hunt through his creation of it in sculpture and painting. In its most complex form, traditional art may be illustrated by the Byzantine school or the imagery of Tibetan Buddhism. In both cases the efficacy of the religious image depends on its being made in accordance with the rules of proportion, color, and arrangement calculated to insure the supernatural aspect of the thing represented. Its power is strengthened by the inclusion of magic emblems. In a traditional art, whether we are concerned with portraits, landscapes, religious images, or birds and animals, the artist's point of view is never realistic, but conceptual, in that he intends to represent the most essential or typical aspects of things as the mind knows them, rather than as the eye sees them. The aim is to represent a universal and recognizable symbol, rather than a facsimile of an actual object. It is not only permissible but necessary to draw a head in profile with an eye in full-face, because these are the most characteristic aspects of these features. In portraying a river landscape the traditional artist may be expected to represent the stream by a series of wavy lines. The fishes in the water would be drawn in profile, and the birds above it with their wings outspread, because these are the attitudes that everyone recognizes as the most typical of fishes and birds.

Whereas traditional art is almost invariably anonymous, and the painter or sculptor a dedicated craftsman, the nontraditional artist is an individual who uses art as an expression of his own personal moods or as a means for displaying his own technical virtuosity. In nontraditional periods artists will express themselves in realistic terms because their whole belief and experience are centered on the material world. The term, nontraditional art, is usually assigned to all work beginning with the Renaissance in Europe when the artist strove to record the outward appearances of nature rather than the underlying spirit operating behind the façade of actuality. Although some critics, for their own sincere metaphysical convictions, urge a return to traditional standards and condemn all nontraditional art as abnormal and degenerate, theirs is an extreme view. Post-Renaissance art is the valid expression of a period in which science replaces tradition. Science here refers to the intellectual submission of all phenomena to general laws governing their appearances and functions on an empirical basis. The fact is that both of these points of view toward art are equally valid and indeed inevitable for the times and societies that produced them. We cannot say that one is better than the other.

It will become apparent to the reader that in traditional art what many would call an unrealistic or distorted representation of nature was necessary for the peculiar spiritual aim the artist had in mind; in other words, the lack of naturalism in a medieval painting or an Indian statue of the Gupta Period (350–600) is not necessarily an indication of technical incompetence. Artists made their representations as "real" as they wanted, depending on the idea the work of art was destined to express.

The distinction between the two types of expression is often extremely tenuous, and, if most of the works reproduced in this book appear to belong to the traditional category, this does not indicate a preference by the author but is the result of the persistence of this point of view in the East until comparatively modern times. Many other examples, like certain Chinese bird-and-flower paintings or even early Indian sculpture which appear to be realistic, are, in actuality, traditional, since the artist is concerned with suggesting the inner life or vitality of his subject: he utilizes the natural form to represent the inner spirit—to paraphrase a Chinese aesthetic canon, "He paints the idea and not merely the shape."

TECHNIQUES IN PAINTING

The Western paintings considered in this book were executed in a variety of media, such as *fresco, oil, tempera,* and *water color.* The materials and processes involved in some of these methods are entirely comparable with techniques developed in the Orient; others are totally different from any Far Eastern mode, so that a short account of these media and their characteristics would seem to be an appropriate part of the introduction to the analysis of individual works of art.

Fresco in the true sense of the word is wall painting in water color on wet plaster or mortar, so that the colors sink into the surface and with its drying become an immortal part of the wall's fabric. This technique, which for obvious reasons requires great breadth of handling is represented in this book by Ambrogio Lorenzetti's *Good Government* (Chapter Two, 1). It has no counterpart in the Orient where wall paintings, like European *fresco secco*,[1] were always executed on a dry wall surface, with the result that, although a certain monumentality is imposed by their function as mural decorations, they hardly differ in technique from work done on paper or silk. The pictures discussed

[1] *Buon fresco* was a term used by Italian artists to define true fresco and to distinguish this process from *fresco secco*—painting on a dry wall surface.

in Chapter One(3) and Chapter Two(2) are examples of this type in Central Asia and China.

In tempera painting, as practiced in the Middle Ages and the Renaissance, the colors, ground from various earths, minerals, and vegetable substances, are mixed with water and yolk of egg as an adherent. The surface is usually *gesso* or plaster of Paris on a wooden panel. The medium enforces a rather meticulous building up of areas in the picture in multiple touches of the brush, without the possibility of the breadth and richness of handling that may be achieved in oil. For this reason tempera paintings in their hardness and dryness of definition may be described as colored drawings. Sometimes tempera is combined with glazes or thin washes of transparent oil paint. The paintings discussed in Chapter One(5, 6, 7, 12), Chapter Two(2, 3), and Chapter Three(8) are illustrations of pure tempera or tempera combined with oil glaze. Such pictures, by reason of their rather precise restriction to contour line and color, approximate the effect of many Oriental paintings, in which the forms are presented essentially in terms of line and color either applied flat or modeled in relief.

Oil painting, as the definition implies, means that the colors are mixed with oil. The artist has a choice of using the medium in a glazing technique, or in what is described as *direct painting*. In glazing, a number of transparent coats of pigment thinly mixed with oil are successively applied over the original drawing which may or may not be executed in tempera. Rich effects of luminosity and tone are possible through this method of superimposed transparent layers of color. Affected by the precise definition of shapes and shadows in the original drawing, this method often has something of the smoothness and hardness of tempera. In direct painting, the artist picks up touches of pure pigment with his brush to apply to the canvas. The paint, which has the consistency of tooth paste or soft butter, may be spread in smooth areas of color in which the strokes of the brush are invisible. The painter may also apply the pigment in many separate strokes or sweeps of the brush to the panel or canvas; in this latter method he paints the picture in terms of separate brushstrokes and in terms of the texture of the pigment itself. Often the *impasto* or pigment surface is built up to a veritable incrustation of paint on the canvas, so that its very thickness or thinness is exploited in the interests of suggesting effects of light, color, and variegated texture. In this method, too, the pattern of brushstrokes and the texture of the paint itself enters into the total aesthetic impression that the painting makes on us. Examples of oil

painting, showing the smoother employment of the medium, are discussed in Chapter Two(6, 7).

In water-color painting the actual pigments of mineral or vegetable
origin are compounded with a gum or glycerine base so that they are
soluble in water. Water color may be used to color neatly and precisely
the different areas of a drawing in pencil or ink. Because of its extremely fluid and transparent nature, the medium may also be used for
effects of great freedom and brilliance impossible to achieve in oil or
tempera. Flowing washes and brushstrokes are combined to define the
forms in the picture and to provide an aesthetic attraction in the pattern and harmony of their arrangement on the paper. Thanks to the
transparency of the colors, the whiteness of the paper itself may be exploited to confer an added brilliance to the technique. Water colors
representing the freer modern employment of the medium are mentioned in Chapter Two(5, 8) and Chapter Four(2); the Western examples described in Chapter Two(5) and Chapter Three(1, 2, 3) provide illustrations of water color primarily used as a means of coloring
sketches and drawings.

It is obvious from the descriptions in the foregoing paragraphs that
Western paintings in water color, tempera, or tempera and oil glaze
provide the nearest counterparts to the techniques of Far Eastern paint-
ting, in which the minimum employment of line, brushstroke, and
color fulfills the artist's maximum aesthetic needs.

A word in general should also be said about the technique of the
Far Eastern paintings to be discussed in relation to their Western
counterparts. Even the very earliest surviving examples of Chinese and
Japanese painting are executed on silk or paper, either in monochrome
ink or in a combination of ink line and opaque water-color pigment.
Depending on the artist and the period, the painting could be either
precise or extremely free in execution. Ink and colors are applied with
a brush which, in the hand of the Oriental artist, is at once pen or pencil and an instrument of great subtlety for the application of washes
in ink or tone. As will be explained in later chapters, the separate brushstrokes combine to give structure to the forms, and in their pattern impart vivacity and harmony to the painting. The very fragility of the
surface and the medium rendered impossible the achievement of the
rich effects of color and texture obtainable in the Western technique
of oil painting. As will become apparent in the analysis of individual
paintings, such effects were incompatible not only with the Oriental
artist's medium but also with the ideas he sought to express. By the

same token the suggestion of texture and light by the variegated thickness and thinness of oil colors on canvas has no equivalent in Far Eastern practice, so that the writer has avoided the selection of later European paintings in which this element of technical manipulation of the
pigment dominates the painting.

Chapter One

The Human Figure

THE representation of man and man's activity has occupied artists of the East and West since the very beginning of time. It could be stated categorically that the representation of the human figure in painting and sculpture vastly outnumbers that of any other subject in art. The theme is so vast that some arbitrary subdivisions must be made to present it with clarity in a book of this type. It is proposed, therefore, to divide this chapter into three parts: (A) The Single Figure, (B) The Portrait, and (C) The Religious Image. It is obvious, of course, that even this division will result in some overlapping, since certain paintings or statues that may be classified as portraits—that is, portrayals of specific individuals—also served as objects of worship. The same is true of certain of the single figures chosen for analysis.

Portraiture, both in the East and West, may be divided into two types of presentation: one, in which the artist is concerned with making a completely realistic recording of the outward appearance of the individual features of the sitter; the

other, in which he has sought to reveal the inner or ghostly aspect of an
individual with the result that some portraits are so spiritualized that
they might be mistaken for religious images. It is obvious, of course,
that this separation is a very arbitrary one since these two approaches
can often be found combined in a single work of art.

Since Western man has always been entranced with his own image,
the human figure in the West has always appealed to artists as a beautiful subject in itself, its beauty to be revealed in terms of muscular
structure, action, the revelation of emotion through expression or pose,
or simply as an always endearing subject that could be exploited for
the purposes of all kinds of design. Perhaps the chief link between
Eastern and Western art in this category is the use of the human figure
to reveal the imagined shapes of the gods. Whereas in the Greek tradition the very idealized perfection of the physical attributes of an image
were sufficient to suggest the divine beauty of a god, in the East the
emphasis has always been on the creation of a supernatural ideal, often
presented in terms only abstractly related to any actual physical body
or its proportions.

The worship of the human body as a beautiful, disciplined mechanism, as the home of the human spirit, and as a reflection of divine beauty
is the most familiar artistic reflection of the Greek view of life and has
never lost its hold on the tradition of the West. The connotation of
aliveness and action that could be revealed in the mastery of the anatomy of the body occupied the Greek artist from earliest times, as did
the problems of muscular articulation, balance, and proportion necessary to confer dignity and beauty on the representation of the shape
of man in art.

This approach to the portrayal of man's image is totally different
from that of the Indian artist. There has never been the slightest prudery
in the representation of naked bodies in India. In Indian art the human
figure is not pictured for its own sake, nor with any interest in the
precise articulation of the muscular structure in any scientific manner.
The nude figure in Indian art is used to suggest the sensuality of fertility spirits or the supreme yogic control of a Jain ascetic, by means
at once appropriately abstract and specific. As a general rule, Indian
artists with no interest in anatomy per se carved figures to suggest the
warmth and fullness of flesh or the presence of enlivening breath or
prāṇa by their abstract manipulation of the swelling interlocking planes
of which the body is composed. The resulting image need not corre-
spond precisely to any human prototype, but is composed according to

canons of proportion calculated to endow it with a more than mortal impressiveness and beauty.

In the Far East the representation of the human figure in early times had a predominantly didactic function of illustrating examples of ethical Confucian behavior or historical episodes, subjects which, since they obviously depend on human actions, could not be shown in any other way. It is not the beauty of the figures, but the beauty of the moral that is important. Although in certain periods the Chinese have been interested in the use of the human figure as an exercise in calligraphic brushwork or nicety of definition in terms of line and wash, the organic or athletic beauty of the body, as a revelation of physical loveliness, has never figured in Chinese art. In the Orient, only the Japanese, with their infinite curiosity and receptivity to foreign fashions, have shown an occasional interest in the nude, and even then the indigenous sense for the grotesque removes these performances from the idealistic Western point of view.

A. THE SINGLE FIGURE

1. *Apollo and Ascetic*

If a typical Jain statue of a nude ascetic (figure 2) and any one of the Apollos or *kouroi* (figure 1) of the archaic period of Greek sculpture were placed side by side, one might reach the superficial conclusion that both are the products of the same environment or at least derived from a common prototype. Neither of these suppositions is valid, and yet something certainly can be said in explanation of this resemblance and also about the essential differences that separate the two conceptions.

The numerous examples of nude statues of kouroi that have been found all over the Greek world and may be dated from the seventh to the fifth centuries B.C. have certain traits in common, in spite of regional differences in technique and material. All are standing in a rigidly frontal position with arms pressed close to the sides and one foot advanced to ensure a firmer stance. Their resemblance to, and probable derivation from, Egyptian prototypes was noted by Diodorus of Sicily, who stated that the Pythian Apollo of Samos "resembled Egyptian works with his arms stretched stiffly down his sides and his legs separated in a stride."

The passage from Diodorus, explaining the Egyptian method of arriving at the proper proportions for statues, states that the sculptors

began by "dividing the structure of the entire body into twenty-one
parts and one-fourth in addition,[1] they express in this way the complete figure in its symmetrical proportions." This is a type of canon
based not on the physical proportions of actual human beings, but on
the employment of an entirely abstract or mathematical modulus calculated to produce an appropriately abstract or mathematical perfection
in the image. Over and beyond these connections with the studio practice of Memphis or Thebes, the Greek kouroi are completely original
conceptions: instead of the frozen rigidity of Egyptian figures, the
kouroi are imbued with a feeling of pent-up vitality that expresses itself
in the tension of the clenched fists and the implication of movement
in the striding legs. These statues, in the untrammeled abstraction of
the bodily form that yet denotes an aliveness and throbbing virility, are
the "perfect expression of ideal youthful manhood, conceived by the
aristocratic Hellenic society of archaic times." [2] A feeling of youthful
manly strength is implied in an abstract, rather than a realistic fashion,
by the athletic ideal of proportion with massive shoulders tapering to
a wasplike waist, in the litheness of the form, and, in the linear conventions implying the tautly stretched tendons of the frame, an emphasis on muscular strength.

The main points of resemblance between the Greek kouros and a
Jain figure of a *tirthankara* or saint lie in the suggestion of heroic, superhuman stature in the completely nude body by the enormous exaggeration of the width of shoulder and narrowness of waist and in the general similarity of the frontal pose with the arms extended down the
sides. In the case of the Jain figures there is no need even to speculate on
the possibility of an Egyptian influence producing this parallel form in
India; the earliest Jain statues, probably not made until the fashion for
the anthropomorphic representation of Gautama had been established
by Buddhism in the second century A.D., date from a period centuries
after the sculptural tradition of ancient Egypt had vanished in the dust.
It will become apparent that, just like the kouroi, the Jain images were
made to fulfill a specific religious need. In the process of their making,
certain devices rather similar to those used by the Greek sculptor were
independently evolved to express the fundamental nature of the conception, and it is this that accounts for the seemingly close but actually
superficial resemblance.

[1] The one-fourth of a unit was presumably left for the hair or headdress, so
that the actual measurement extended from the hairline of the brow to the feet.
[2] Georg H. Karo, *Greek Personality in Archaic Sculpture* (Cambridge: Harvard University Press, 1948), p. 105.

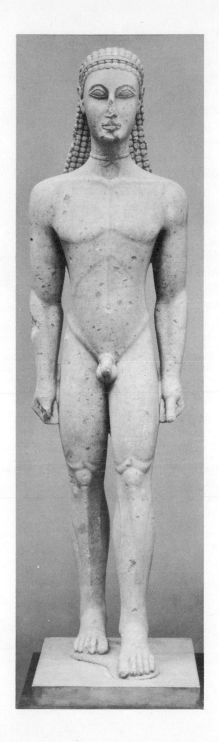

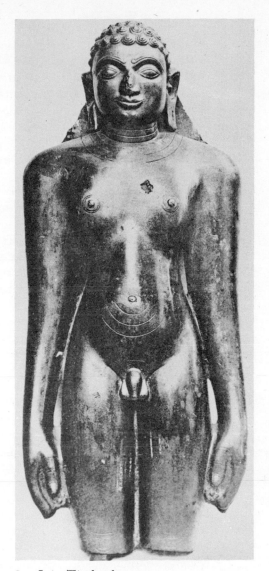

2. *Jain Tirthankara*

1. *Statue of Apollo or Kouros*

The naked figures of Jain saints represent the act of *kayotsarga* or dismissing the body, the attainment of a depth of yogic trance in which the practitioner is completely withdrawn from all earthly distractions, so that some Jain patriarchs are said to have been entirely impervious to vines twining around their limbs and ant-hills growing round their feet; it is a state of suspended animation amounting to a suspension of all bodily function, a state in which, by the power of concentration, the fleshly body is cleansed to a point of alabastrine purity and assumes a perfection free of the dross of tangible matter.

In the figuration of such a concept the Indian sculptor employed certain techniques that were the common property of all craftsmen employed in making religious images in India. In order to convey the impression that we are looking at a superman, spiritually as well as anatomically above ordinary mortals, the body is composed on the metaphorical basis used for the making of Buddha images: we can easily recognize the leonine body, the arms tapering like an elephant's trunk, the thighs like plantains, as well as the lotiform eyes and other ideal abstractions for the features. The canon of proportion is an abstract one, too, composed of nine *thalams*, the distance from brow to chin, for the total height of the statue.

In the use of a mathematical system of measurement to ensure an appropriately ideal abstraction, the parallel to the Greek figure is a legitimate one. But in the Indian statue these means are dedicated to quite different ends. The Jain figure represents a spiritual, not an athletic ideal. Its nudity is conditioned by asceticism, not pride in physical beauty. Whereas in the Apollo the emphasis is on muscular structure, in the body of the Jain ascetic there is a complete suppression of muscular or skeletal structure even in an abstract way. The body and limbs are composed of a number of smooth, uninterrupted convex surfaces or planes, the swelling roundness of which not only connotes the perfection attained by breath control, but, in the reduction of the anatomical structure itself to the simplest possible surfaces, indicates that the form is composed of "some supraterrestrial unearthly substance."[1]

The stance of the Jain figure is intended to suggest the supernally motionless state of a being withdrawn in the timeless serenity of yoga, not the athletic vigor implied in the tension of the Greek statue. Even the hands extended down the legs suggest the infinite relaxation of trance in contrast to the surging vitality of the clenched fists of the kouros.

[1] H. Zimmer, *Philosophies of India* ("Bollingen Series XXVI" [New York: Pantheon Press, 1951]), p. 212.

Surprisingly similar abstract means are used, on the one hand to
suggest youthful beauty throbbing with physical life, and on the other
hand a body as a symbol of spirit and an expression of complete withdrawal from all material being and the round of birth and death.

2. *The Male Nude*

Almost from the moment that it was unearthed at the ancient site
of Harappā, the little limestone torso illustrated in figure 4 has been
compared to the finest accomplishments of Greek sculpture. Some critics have even suggested that it must be assigned to a period when the
influence of Hellenic art on India could be invoked to account for the
carver's mastery of anatomical form. The fact remains that this figurine,
excavated under scientific conditions, belongs to the Prehistoric or
Indus Valley Period and is to be dated in the later third millennium B.C.
It will become apparent, too, on comparison with a typical Greek representation of the nude, that the figure is completely Indian in character and execution and, in a sense, diametrically opposed to the Hellenic ideal. As a Greek counterpart for this Indian masterpiece we may
select a terra cotta figurine of a *diadoumenos*, an athlete binding his
fillet, copied from a bronze statue by Polyclitus.

Polyclitus belongs to the great period of Greek sculpture, the Age
of Pericles (450–400 B.C.), and is generally ranked second only to the
great Phidias. He was the leading sculptor in the school of Argos. The
accounts by ancient writers tell us that, although versatile in subject
matter, his fame rested chiefly on his statues of athletes. Although no
original work by Polyclitus has survived, a number of later copies,
both Greek and Roman, serve to give us an idea of his style in sculpture.

In the account of his work by Greek and Roman critics we learn
that Polyclitus was actuated by a desire for perfection in proportion,
the creation of human figures which, in their harmonious relation of
the parts to the whole, would excel or improve on the accidental and
varied beauty of individual human beings. Polyclitus formulated a
canon of proportions which exercised a great influence on later generations of Greek artists. Although this system of measurement is sometimes described as consisting merely of a ratio of seven heads to the
total height of the body, it was obviously a more complete and
complicated approach than this simple ratio would indicate: it was a
humanistic harmony of proportion based on the relationship of each
part of the body to all the other parts and to the whole. This is something quite different from the system of measurement followed in the
archaic period which was based *a priori* on a division of the entire

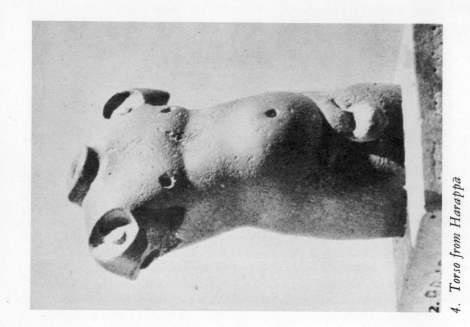

4. *Torso from Harappā*

3. *Diadoumenos*

stature of the figure into a fixed number of numerical units in much
the same way as the archaic concept of the cosmos was fitted into a
preconceived geometric scheme. Polyclitus' efforts to create a norm of
beauty parallel the direction of the philosophy and science of his time
in its attempt to simplify the complexity of all experience and phenomena into easily comprehensible and concrete terms.

In the Polyclitan ideal of the nude male body, the weight is on the
left leg and the right arm is flexed, while the right leg and left arm are
relaxed, so that the statue achieves a wonderful balance in weight and
tension and a suggestion of lithe activation. The head and the torso and
muscular divisions of chest and abdomen all have a square-cut cubic
shape collectively suggesting a stocky ideal of beauty. This repetition
of the solid shapes that comprise the body in itself imposes an abstract
harmony on the statue and is an approach far removed from the literal
copying of a model. The representation of the parts of the body and their
interrelation is, of course, anatomically correct—some Polyclitan statues
even show the veins beneath the skin—but carving reduces the surface to
a succession of smooth and softly interlocking planes without the least
suggestion of texture, so that we recognize the abstraction and are
never disturbed by any attempt to imitate literally flesh and blood in
marble or bronze.

Although it is impossible to tell the exact iconographic significance
of the nude image from Harappā, it seems almost certain that it must
have been intended as a deity of some sort. In its present damaged con-
dition no recognizable attributes remain; nor is there any explanation
for the curious circular depressions in the clavicle region. In the
Harappā torso there is no attempt to suggest the human body by emphasizing the muscular structure that was the particular concern of the
naturalistically minded Greek sculptors of the fourth century B.C. and
later. On the contrary, this statuette is completely Indian in the sculptor's realization of the essential image, a symbolic rather than descrip-
tive representation of anatomy, in which the articulation of the body is
realized in broad convex planes of modeling. The one quality which
may be discerned here that is peculiar to many later Indian examples
of plastic art is the suggestion of an inner tension that seems to threaten
to push out and burst the taut outer layer of skin. Actually, this is a
technical device by which the sculptor revealed the existence of the
breath or *prāṇa* filling and expanding the vessel of the body. The fact
that the figure appears potbellied is, therefore, iconographically completely right and truthful. It is not intended as a caricature in any
sense, since this distension resulting from yogic breath control was re-

garded as an outward sign of both material and spiritual well-being. We have in this statuette, too, what is certainly the earliest exhibition of the Indian sculptor's skill in producing not only a sense of plastic volume but also in representing the soft quality of the flesh. This is not a literal imitation, such as one finds in Western sculpture, but a suggestion of fleshiness by such properly sculptural and abstract devices as the interlocking of the smooth and softly modeled convex planes of the torso and the exaggeration of the depth of the navel.

The anatomically accurate description of the bony structure in its envelope of muscles and skin that characterizes the Greek statue is by no means suggested in the Indian torso. The entire emphasis is on the body rendered immaculate by the very smoothness of its surface and without irregularities to disturb its alabastrine perfection. In many respects this statuette already anticipates those descriptions of the Indian hero which came to be applied in defining the perfection of the anatomy of the Buddha: "the seven parts of the body . . . rounded and full," "neither veins nor bones are seen," "the shoulders and arms are perfectly round," and so on.[1] It anticipates the technique of countless images of Indian gods made centuries after its fashioning in the third millennium B.C. By these same tokens it already establishes the essential differences that were forever to separate the Indian from the Hellenic point of view toward the representation of gods and heroes in art.

3. *Aphrodite and Yakshi*

A comparison of the "Aphrodite of Cyrene" (figure 5) with the figure of a *yakshī* from Sāñchī (figure 6) presents us with the problem of how a sculptor, limited to the subject of the nude female form, produces a cult image which by reason of its iconography was required to have a definitely provocative and sensuous appeal. The two statues illustrate the completely opposed means by which it was possible to attain such an ideal. The Greek Aphrodite represents its achievement in perfected human terms; the Indian demigoddess, in nonhumanistic or abstract terms. It is obvious that Aphrodite as a personification of love and beauty had to be represented as a beautiful woman.

In the sculpture of the great period of Greek art, as illustrated by the Polyclitan figure of Chapter One(2), we sense an Olympian nobility and serenity in the heroic forms of the gods. In these statues of the fifth century, abstraction in smooth and sharply demarcated planes dominates realistic approximation to a human model, and for this reason

[1] A. Grünwedel, *Buddhist Art in India*, trans. Agnes C. Gibson (London: Bernard Quaritch, 1901), pp. 161–162.

6. *Yakshī*

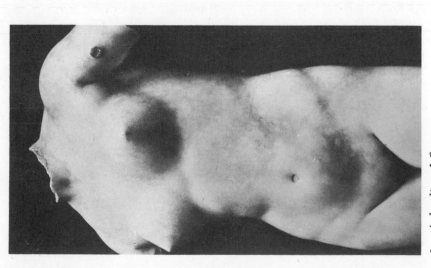

5. *Aphrodite of Cyrene*

the sculptured figures of the Parthenon achieve an ideality suggesting a superior human race in stone. The "Aphrodite of Cyrene," although certainly one of the loveliest fragments of antique sculpture, belongs to a different and aesthetically less distinguished plastic tradition. If we were to formulate a purist definition of sculpture at its finest, we would specify a style in which the form realized in stone still reveals its origin in that material; this style would be governed by underlying geometric shapes that remove it from reality so that the head still suggests the sphere, the limbs and torso, the cylinder. This is a standard, typified in different ways by the Parthenon marbles and by the Indian statue to be analyzed in this chapter. This is, of course, an oversimplification of the sculptor's problem, but the fact remains that the more he departs from this norm of perfection in the direction of imitative naturalism, the less truly sculptural his work becomes.

The "Aphrodite of Cyrene" is the end of the Greek sculptor's search for realistic representation. It belongs to a period (*ca.* third century B.C.) when approximation to human standards of loveliness was a necessity in order to make the Olympian gods more imminent and tangible than was possible in the heroic shapes bestowed on them in the age of Phidias.[1] The result is a statue in which the sculptor, by his use of the fine grain of the marble and the lustrous polish imparted to its surface, endeavors to persuade the beholder that he has produced a veritable counterfeit of flesh. This effect is achieved not only by the presentation of the goddess in actual human proportion and by the definition of every captivating undulation in the topography of the beautiful body, but also by the very softness and delicacy of carving the manifold planes that comprise the fleshly envelope. The statue in its surface treatment presents a marvelous illusion of a real body, defined by the wonderfully subtle shadows that both model the form and confer an almost translucent aspect to its surface.

The result is, of course, that, in comparison with the limited realism of the Parthenon sculpture, the sense of the stone material is destroyed in the attempt to persuade us that it is indeed the substance of a living body. The impossibility of such a facsimile is against the permanence of the illusion. As suggested above, the overemphasis on texture and surface partly destroys the validity of the carving as a work of sculpture. This is the result of the Greek sculptor's abandonment of the appropriately abstract and truly plastic treatment of form, as in the style

[1] This same contrast can be made in the Greek drama between Sophocles' characters conceived as models of heroic human nature and Euripides' creation of men and women as they are.

of the fifth century, in favor of the labored manipulation of surfaces to secure the novelty of realistic erotic appeal.

The Indian statue of a yakshī is datable in the first century B.C. From the point of view of provocative sensuality and actual fleshliness, it appears at first to bear a superficial similarity to the Aphrodite, but it is a statue composed according to totally different iconographic and technical ideals. The yakshī is among the oldest of Indian divinities whose worship extends to the pre-Buddhist and pre-Hindu periods of Indian civilization, when a primitive nature worship was the universal popular cult. The yakshīs could be described as dryads associated with the blossoming and fruition of trees. By extension they came to be regarded as universal fertility spirits, responsible not only for the fecundity of growing things but for the fertility of their human devotees as well. It is not unlikely that in the very early period these tree spirits took on the attributes and powers of the universal mother who, under various names, was worshiped all over the ancient world. By reason of her association with the powers of generation it was appropriate that the yakshī should be endowed with the provocative feminine attributes bestowed on Cybele and Aphrodite. There the resemblance ceases, because the erotic attractions of the Indian goddess are suggested within terms essentially abstract and plastic. The Indian sculptor was never interested in the achievement of the kind of surface realism that was a continuing challenge to the Greek artist. The implication of the Indian goddess's procreative powers is contained in the exaggeration of the globular pendulousness of the breasts which appear like "golden jars," [1] and there is a corresponding frank emphasis on the widespread hips and pudenda. The representation of the body at first glance gives the impression of swelling fleshly fullness, just as definitely sensuous as the anatomy of the Aphrodite. There is no attempt here, however, to suggest that the stone material has been magically transmuted into flesh, but only a connotation of the quality of flesh in terms of stone. The interlocking of the subtly swelling convex planes that define the bosom, abdomen, and pelvis serve to demonstrate, in appropriately abstract terms, the roundness and fullness and warmth of an actual body without in any way negating the nature of the medium. Such devices as the constriction of the abdomen by the tight beaded belt further this abstract illusion by the creation of an overlapping fold of flesh around the circumference of the girdle. The uninterrupted smoothness and deliberately exaggerated roundness of the consecutive planes that define the

---

[1] Aśvaghosa, *Buddhacarita*, IV, 35. Cf. A. K. Coomaraswamy in *Bulletin of the Museum of Fine Arts*, Boston, December 1929, p. 94.

torso suggest that quality of expansiveness, that same inward pneumatic quality that distinguishes Indian sculpture from the sculpture of any other race.

To summarize, the essential difference between these two images, both dedicated to reminding the devotee of his own capacity for erotic enjoyment and procreation, is that the Greek statue seeks to achieve this end by a very frank and literal imitation of an actual body in marble, while the image of the yakshī fulfills the same iconographic function by means that are essentially abstract, and by the same token entirely plastic and appropriate to the medium.

4. *Two Giants of Painting*

The one artist who has been extolled by Chinese critics of every period as the foremost master in all classes of subject matter was Wu Tao-tzŭ, who lived in the eighth century A.D. As early as the end of the T'ang Dynasty he was ranked in the highest or inspired grade and is said to have been the master of all Six Principles of Painting.

The so-called Six Principles of Painting were set down first by the critic, Hsieh Ho, in the fourth century A.D. as a recension of even older traditions. These Principles or Branches of the art are not hard and fast rules that a painter was bound to observe, but rather standards of perfection in performance toward which all painters could aspire. Later in the history of Chinese criticism, painters were ranked according to their degree of mastery of these canons, particularly of the First Principle. By this the chief aim of the artist was to imbue his painted forms with the feeling of vitality or spirit-harmony in accordance with the special kind of movement, rhythm, or life characteristic of all things in the world of nature. The remaining principles were in a sense subservient to this final aim and included the proper use of brushwork, ink, compositional arrangement, color, and the intelligent copying of classic prototypes.

Wu Tao-tzŭ is said to have been possessed with a kind of divine energy. The onlookers who gathered to see him complete one of his compositions testify that he swirled his brush with the force of a whirlwind and by the aid of a supernatural power. His paintings, we are told, were so infused with the breath of life that the creatures of his brush threatened to come alive upon the painted surface; and his draped figures were caught in billowing folds that seem to swirl and move as though a wind were in them.

Needless to say, no originals from Master Wu's brush have come down to us. The one reflection of his work that still survives to give us some idea of the stupendous power and freedom of his brush is a stone engraving, after a drawing of a flying devil by Wu Tao-tzŭ, preserved at Chu Yang, Hopei Province (figure 8). This stone engraving is probably a faithful replica of a painting done entirely in black outline in the so-called *pai hua* technique. In contrast to the precise definition in even and unbroken contour lines that characterizes the Chinese figure drawing of earlier centuries, we have here a design filled with tremendous movement and energy, and one in which, for the first time in the development of painting in China, the subtle thinning and thickening of the lines by the moving brush makes for a powerful and plastic realization of the form. The tremendously dynamic articulation of the anatomy conveys the feeling that the figure is literally swelling with the pressure of pent-up energy. Combined with the flame-like hair and the swirling movement of the flying draperies, the superhuman vitality of the figure itself presents a design of demoniacal heroic force.

The only possible comparison in Western art for this suggestion of superhuman energy in pictorial terms is to be found in the paintings and drawings of Michelangelo (1475–1564). Michelangelo, as in the drawing selected for comparison (figure 7), also created figures imbued with a divine energy by endowing them with superhuman physical proportions and by a torsion of the bodies calculated to strengthen the feeling of dynamic movement. He achieved this effect by the exaggeration of the size and tension of the swollen muscles to express the idea of Herculean physical power. It can be said of him that he invented a kind of superhuman anatomy based partly on human, partly on Graeco-Roman models, which he felt was only proper to express the heroic stature of the beings with which he peopled the Bible story. Michelangelo's violence and dynamic contortion appear as the outward manifestation of an internal conflict of forces mutually stimulating and paralyzing one another. These tortured bodies are thought to represent the conflict in Michelangelo himself, between his medieval Christian belief and the pagan form and thought of his day, or the allegory of a soul held in bondage by its natural desires. These titan forms are typical of the West, in that they are called from the vasty deep of the soul of an individual genius and are expressions of his unique reaction to the world. Wu Tao-tzŭ's forms are not so much expressions of an individual's own state of emotion, but universal graphic portrayals of the flux of the world movement in action, the force that bends the grasses and steers the stars in their courses, the force that sucks up the tide and breathes the whirlwind. It is, in simple words, the breath of life, expressed in the most powerfully imagined pictorial terms, for the trans-

7. *Libyan Sybil*

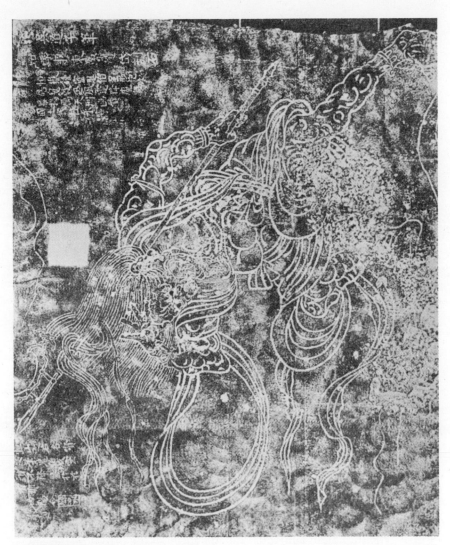

8. Flying Devil

mission of which the artist is only a kind of gifted agent acting in response to irresistible inspiration.

Wu Tao-tzŭ's supernatural creature is not based on any human or classic models, but is an almost abstract creation, made up of wonderfully articulated and appropriate brushstrokes which, by their intrinsic character and shapes, rather than by their adherence to the forms of real anatomy, are calculated to express the demoniacal strength of a being from the other world. The strokes of Michelangelo's pen in parallel lines reinforcing the contours of muscles, or in cross-hatchings suggesting the strokes of the chisel in his sculpture, are comparable to the brushstrokes of Wu Tao-tzŭ; but they are dedicated to evoking the plastic form on the paper, almost as though the artist were painfully disengaging it from a block of marble, and, as we have seen, the ultimate end is an expression at once humanistic and intensely personal. Wu Tao-tzŭ's design has no humanistic or subjective intent; it can only be described as an imaginary creation infused with the quality described in the first of the Six Principles: spirit-harmony through life-movement.

B. THE PORTRAIT

5. St. Francis and the Patriarch

What is meant by traditional portraiture may be very well explained by quoting an apocryphal legend of St. John the Evangelist who, when presented with a portrait of himself, remarked:

The portrait is like me, yet not like me but like my fleshly image, for if this painter desireth to draw the very me in a portrait, he will need more than colors and things that are seen with the eye. This that thou hast done is childish and imperfect. Thou hast drawn a dead likeness of the dead.[1]

We have here the expression of an idea growing out of the tenets of Plotinus, that the artist cannot be satisfied with a mere transcription of physical appearance, but must strive to portray the final spiritual or ghostly nature of an individual shining through the prison of the physical body. This same conception of the portrait as revealing the spirit rather than the substance is present in the traditional periods of art in the Far East.

An illustration of this point of view may be found in the religious portraits of Europe and the Orient: a thirteenth-century portrait of St. Francis (figure 9) and a twelfth-century painting of a Buddhist

[1] M. R. James, *The Apocryphal New Testament* (Oxford: Clarendon Press, 1926), pp. 232 ff.

patriarch (figure 10). Both of these pictures in a sense are portraits because they represent historical personages, and each is at the same time
a religious image inviting the worship of the devotee. Neither is, however, a portrait in the sense of an actual physical appearance of a given
individual.

The portrait of St. Francis is one of a number of such panels painted
within fifty years of the saint's death and canonization, so that there is
the possibility, at least, of its being based on an actual likeness made
in the subject's lifetime. The completely frontal pose with the right hand
raised in blessing and the left holding a book was probably deliberately
chosen for its resemblance to the pose of Christ in many earlier examples of panel and mosaic; such a model was useful to the artist for
technical reasons, and for the worshiper its selection identified St. Francis with Christ as symbolized in the Miracle of the Stigmata.

The canon of proportion is an unnatural or abstract one, probably
based on the Byzantine system of nine heads to the total height of the
figure, a ratio intended by the resulting attenuation to impart a feeling
of ghostly, supernatural grandeur to the form, appropriate to the representation of divine personages. The style of the painting itself can be
described as Romanesque. Except for the noting of the peculiar features
of the Franciscan robe, such as the hood and rope girdle, the drapery
is a schematized reduction of an ultimately classical model to a linear
formula, such as we can see in countless representations of Christ
and the saints in the Romanesque fresco and panel painting of all
Europe. The individual lines and striations that compose the drawing are reinforced with a hard, completely arbitrary shading that imparts a suggestion of plasticity to the abstract organization in linear
terms. This same combination of abstract line and shading is used for the
representation of the face. The face itself is a mask composed of individually idealized features with no suggestion of any real articulation
or anatomical structure beyond what is connoted by their juxtaposition.
The mystical and unreal conception is further emphasized by the entirely frontal pose that commands the reverence of the beholder. The
figure is framed in a background of gold leaf. This golden background
implies existence in a spaceless, supernatural ambient and by its luminosity symbolically connotes the ineffable light of Paradise.

Although the figure of St. Francis is a religious image belonging to
a period when all portraits were types rather than individual character-
izations, yet, within the rigid limits of the formula, there are unmistak-
able signs of an attempt to suggest individuality in the features. The
mask is not borrowed from any preëxisting type used for Christ or one

9. *St. Francis of Assisi*

10. *Tendai Patriarch*

of His saints. Such aspects of the face as its emphatic emaciation suggested by the high cheek bones, the deep parentheses of the lines enclosing the mouth, and the suggestion of beard and moustache, might be regarded as reminiscences of an actual person, whose transfigured physical body is presented in a formula associated in the mind of the worshiper with the standard method of painting entirely supernatural beings from the Christian legend. It is this persistence of emphasis on personality which, in earlier centuries, was apparent even in the conventions of Byzantine art that is, perhaps, the most Western aspect of the painting. As a portrait the representation can be called a type, but it is more than this. The main emphasis is, of course, on the transcendent rather than the human quality of the personage, so that it is a portrait of the spirit of St. Francis rather than of his actual appearance. The symbol of the robe, the hieratic proportion and pose, and the haggard mask of the face combine to suggest at once the sanctity and dignity of the canonized friar and the ascetic simplicity of his person and his Order. Such a spiritual portrait could obviously be achieved only by a purposely abstract mode of representation, with the resulting suppressing of any suggestions of corporeal reality.

Comparable to such spiritual effigies in European painting as the St. Francis altarpiece are examples of portraits of saintly personages in Japanese painting. We may choose for analysis and comparison a banner from a series of the Ten Patriarchs of Tendai Buddhism, belonging to the temple of Ichijōji. Tendai Buddhism which, based upon the tenets of the Lotus Sūtra, recognized both the universal and mortal nature of the Buddha, was a sect that was eclectic in the variety of avenues to salvation which it offered to its adherents. Although the pillars of Tendai Buddhism rested on the possibility of Enlightenment through wisdom, good works, or meditation, there were the added possibilities of achieving union with the divine by means of mystical contemplation, the employment of magic gestures and charms, and a reliance on rites and formulas of Indian Vedic origin. It is not surprising, therefore, that the portraits of the hierarchy of Tendai patriarchs should really be representations of these various aspects of the religion, rather than portrayals of actual personages. One of these, the portrait of Memmyō, the Indian Aśvaghosa, is an emblem of the serenity that comes from supreme wisdom and contemplation. Another banner in the series, representing an unidentified patriarch, shows us a man with his face contorted in a paroxysm as he concentrates in a kind of demoniacal frenzy on the recitation of the Mantra or magic spell that invokes the appearance of Bishamon, the Guardian of the North and special protector of the Tendai shrine on Hieizan.

The unidentified Patriarch chosen for illustration here (figure 10) is represented standing in a frontal position, his right hand raised in the Buddhist gesture of reassurance, his left holding a sacred text or *sūtra*. Pose and attribute conform closely to the portrayal of St. Francis, and the figure exerts the same magnetic attraction as it appears to advance like a luminous phantom from the dark silk, arresting the beholder with the beautiful, serene gesture of the hand and the hypnotic force of the concentrated gaze.

As in the case of the portrait of St. Francis, the likeness of the Patriarch must be a posthumous one, and the question of its being based on an earlier picture taken from life is ultimately of even less significance. In accounts of portraiture in the texts of early Chinese painting the emphasis is invariably placed on a painter's ability to present the spirit of the sitter rather than his actual physical appearance. The artist by a sort of clairvoyance is to project into the painting a portrayal of what a man represents rather than what he appears to be. Descriptions like this may leave the reader rather confused as to what exactly differentiates a spiritual portrait from a realistic one; he may even wonder just how the suggestion of such an elusive factor as what a man represents is to be achieved.

In Oriental religious portraits like the present example the effect is gained in part by the painter's drawing a generalized type rather than an individual; that is, the portrayal of the Patriarch with his smooth, massive features, shaven head, and such attributes as his robe and gestures, would be immediately recognizable as a priest in much the same way that the no less generalized portrait of St. Francis symbolized his essential saintly character. Just as the spiritual expressiveness of St. Francis was enhanced by his attitude and gesture taken over from earlier representations of Christ, the spiritual quality of the Buddhist patriarch is intensified by its resemblance in pose and type to the formula for portraying the Buddha himself which, of course, would have been completely familiar to all.

In the final analysis this Japanese banner is a presentation of a holy man concentrating on the mystic formulas of Tendai ritual. The likeness of the saint is painted in a technique of line and flat tone. The line has at once a decorative quality and the function of suggesting the structure of the figure and its garment. The flat, patternized character of the form is heightened by the emphasis on the moving, irregular silhouette against the dark background. At the same time, this figure of massive proportions has a suggestion of an active pneumatic force expanding the form, reminiscent of the technique of Indian sculpture, already mentioned. In this respect, the painted figure has very much the same sense of volume and dynamic power that characterizes Japanese sculpture of the ninth and tenth centuries.

The quality of inner ghostly power in the face is enhanced by the shape of the eyes that approximate the lotiform eyes of Buddhas and Bodhisattvas; the lips are parted as though the sage were intoning a prayer or magic formula. This portrait has something of the almost frightening dynamic character that we associate with the icons of the more fearsome deities of the Buddhist pantheon. The figure of the Patriarch, his face a mask of mystical concentration, his whole body swelling with unreleased energy, seems completely expressive of the dark, mysterious, and foreboding powers of Tendai Buddhism itself. As the altarpiece of St. Francis was intended to reveal the spirit of the saint and his order, his asceticism, humility, and spiritual grandeur, so also was the Tendai portrait a revelation of the tenets of the sect in action rather than a precise record of the appearance of one single patriarch.

6. Profiles

In the history of art in the West and the East, the profile is probably the oldest form of the portrait. This is because the profile is the most typical aspect of the face, a simple image in silhouette which the memory can retain more readily than a frontal or three-quarters view complicated by foreshortening and overlapping planes. The profile view is not one in which we often observe our friends, but it is the one by which we can most easily remember them.

In all the ancient cultures of the Near East—Egypt, Mesopotamia, and Iran—where artists worked within a conceptual rather than a realistic framework of expression, the head is always shown in profile, and, entirely appropriate to this mode of thinking, the eye is drawn in front view; similarly, the body from the waist up is portrayed frontally and the legs, from their most typical aspect, in profile. In this system the whole figure was built up of parts each recorded in its most specific aspect and without regard for its biological articulation in a realistic sense.

Even in later periods, when an essentially naturalistic point of view had replaced the old conceptual approach, the profile still retained its fascination for artists for both the decorative and psychological possi-

11. *Giuliano de' Medici*

12. *Head of Krishna or Indian Prince*

bilities inherent in it. How its employment typified both the Western and Oriental approach to portraiture may be illustrated by a comparison between a portrait by Sandro Botticelli (1444–1510), formerly in the Kaiser Friedrich Museum in Berlin, and a drawing by an artist of the Rājput School in eighteenth-century India.

Painted profile portraits have a distinct relation to profile portraits in low relief in which the sculptor is interested in similar problems of clarification and control of space. Just as the sculptor has to suggest by foreshortening the existence of the multiple planes of the face in a depth of little more than an inch, the painter has to produce the same effect on the flat surface of his panel.

The profile portrait is a definite contribution of fifteenth-century Italy to the history of art in western Europe. In a sense it is the result of the same desire to clarify and simplify the newly apprehended world of reality that we find in so many branches of Renaissance achievement. Florentine artists worked not only from reality but from memory as a means of recording only what was significant and important. Since the profile is a typical memory image, it has about it something of the eternal. It tends to be flat because objects are remembered in their least foreshortened aspect. The profile portrait also recommended itself by reason of the decorative relationship between the contour of the profile and the rectangular shape of the panel, so that a self-contained design was almost automatically achieved. In these portraits, as nowhere else in the history of painting, is there a perfect balance between design and realism.

We may take as an example of the profile portrait in the Florentine Renaissance the portrait of Giuliano de' Medici painted by Sandro Botticelli (figure 11). Botticelli was trained under the pioneers in the scientific development of the laws of realistic representation in art, based on the discoveries or rediscoveries of the laws of perspective, foreshortening, and spatial arrangement. The artist, in other words, belonged to a time when it was possible to express any subject or theme in completely real terms without reliance on the receipts and prescriptions that had determined artistic practice in the Middle Ages. He had all the tools necessary for any kind of representation: it simply remained to be seen what he, as an artist and not an anonymous craftsman, had to say with this equipment. It is here, of course, that the personality and temperament of the individual genius comes in. In Botticelli's case his artistic personality is to be explained by a dualism in his spiritual personality: a devotion to the cult of Neo-Platonism which, in a kind of intellectualized sensuality, saw a revelation of the divine in human physical beauty, opposed to an almost mystical Christianity that, in his last years, led him to espouse the cause of the doomed Savonarola who inveighed against the frivolity and licentiousness of Florentine life. This is obviously a combination of influences which, although seemingly opposed, would lead to an artistic expression of something more than a straightforward presentation of reality. It resulted in the presentation, in realistic and readable form, of the spiritual character—pagan or Christian—that the artist saw behind the physical framework of a particular human entity.

Botticelli belonged to an age of artistic experimentation, in which the possibility of suggesting the tangible existence of form in space through the rediscovered possibilities of light and shade was a source of continuing fascination; even though his principal mode of expression was line, he modeled the form with such a consideration for accuracy of value that the bust stands out on the panel almost as a work in low relief.

By reason of the peculiarities of his own environment and psychology, Botticelli had developed a personal type of face and figure to portray adequately that ideal of ethereal Neo-Platonic beauty, in which he wished to create his imagined evocations of pagan legend, as well as Christian story. It was inevitable that his portraits of real people should be cast in this mould of rarefied perfection, so that, in a sense, all of them are portraits of Botticelli himself. The formula includes an extraordinary precision of linear definition—a chiseling of the features through the very sharpness and clarity of the line that defines them, a fondness for long, attenuated faces with prominent cheekbones and round, apple-like chins, and, inevitably, a ghostly, almost translucent pallor of complexion that actively defines, in physical terms, the spirit within.

The portrait of Giuliano is in reality an incarnation of the age and its painter as well. The features are those of a specific individual, but cast in a mould of Botticelli's making in order to emphasize Giuliano's social station as well as his inner character as the artist saw them. There is a kind of refinement through austerity of presentation: the very simplicity of the costume and its details, the isolation of the head against an icy blue sky that seems to enhance the cold precision and nobility of the features. Although these features themselves may be handsome in a physical way, their beauty is intensified by the sharpness and clarity of their definition, by the very hardness of the contour lines that model the saliencies of the face upon the panel. Botticelli has succeeded in suggesting the inner character of Giuliano as the portrait of a boy whose thoughts turn inward to himself, a spoiled and even cynical representative of an aristocratic class; the slow, sensuous curve of the lips is taken up and repeated in the curve of the eyelid that almost entirely covers the eye, and thereby suggests a brooding, introspective nature. What we have here for the first time, expressed, to be sure, in relatively simple terms, is the artistic revelation of a psychological state. It may have been the introverted nature of Botticelli's own personality that led him to see something sympathetically related to his own state in the subjects of his portraits. This device of the lowered lids and smiling lips, used here to suggest a kind of inner self-satisfaction and haughty aloofness, is used as a sort of cliché to suggest a state of inner beatitude in the masks of Buddha carved by artists in the jungles of Cambodia.

The portrait of Giuliano de' Medici is completely static, with no suggestion of movement to disturb the hard crystalline presentation of the form. The portrait is still composed in nonrealistic fashion, so that we have a profile head joined to a foreshortened bust. In other words, we do not have the feeling of a completely organic synthesis between all parts of the body and empty space that we find in portraits of the High Renaissance.

In India the profile portrait is geographically and traditionally closer to its place of origin, the ancient Near East. So universally favored is this type of portrait both in Mogul and Rājput painting of the sixteenth century and later, that its beginnings in India must be traced to an earlier classic period. Although no examples have survived from the centuries of the Gupta Period (350–700), literary evidence points to the popularity of portraits by both professional and amateur artists: one of the keys of the plot of the famous play, *Sakuntala*, is a painting of the king's beloved.

A beautiful example of Rājput portraiture is an eighteenth-century drawing from Jaipur, in the collection of the Metropolitan Museum, usually labelled "Krishna," but most likely a portrait of a contemporary prince (figure 12). This large drawing was intended as a cartoon for a wall painting and is executed in precise linear definition filled in with flat areas of color. In the actual delineation of the features, there is a reminiscence of the old Indian metaphorical mode of representing the parts of the body and features in shapes suggested by similar forms in the world of nature, so that the eyes are lotiform and the brows have a bowlike curvature. Again, following the age-old conceptual approach, the artist presents the head in profile and the body in frontal view. Rājput portraits never attempt the suggestion of individual personality in realistic terms, so that in this respect the Indian drawing is diametrically opposed to the aims of Botticelli's picture of Giuliano. There is no psychological interpretation beyond the animation and sensuous beauty within the essentially linear character of the drawing. This effect is achieved partly by the repetition of shapes in the long, tremulous curves of brows, eyes, and lips, partly by the exotic refinement of the features themselves. A very slight shading contributes a suggestion of softness and relief to the face. The draughtsmanship has a wiry elegance which admirably defines the sharp contours of the face, the supple fullness of the youthful bust. Line is employed with a decorative intent in the drawing of the locks of hair. These black serpentine accents stand out so that they have an aesthetic attraction that might almost seem independent of the picture as a whole. Actually, these moving lines, together with the drawing of the bending jewels and feathers of the turban, are an integral part of the design; they serve to relieve the static character of the figure as a whole. As we have seen, a use of similar moving line by European artists like Botticelli resulted in effects both decorative and expressive of the psychological character of the subject, whereas in the Rājput drawing these lines are only parts of an aesthetically moving arrangement that remains completely anonymous—telling us nothing of the character of either subject or painter. In this respect, the painting is an illustration of the complete suppression of individuality in the tradition of Indian craftsmanship. At the same time it reveals to us how, in Indian art, portraits, just as much as representations of gods, are symbols of general ideas, a point of view in which reference to the particular has no place.

This is a late and mannered example of a classic Indian style that can be traced back to the masterpieces of the Gupta Period at Ajantā. In place of the breadth and vitality of these early examples, the effect in the present work is achieved by the very delicacy of the drawing of details of costume and jewels; the face itself is just another detail in a design which, in the collective definition of exquisite minutiae, evokes a feeling of sensuous elegance and aristocratic refinement.

7. *King and Shogun*

In the Western world before the appearance of a philosophical and religious point of view that stressed the importance of the individual rather than the universal, there was no need for portraits which were records of human beings and not merely types or effigies. Toward the end of the thirteenth century the philosophical and social climate in Europe was appropriate for such a development of portraiture. Among the many factors contributing to this, we may mention the rise of empirical science with its emphasis on the experience of reality, and the importance of the individual in his relationship to the world and to God in the Franciscan doctrine. Also the revival of the concept of fame as an inheritance from the antique played its part in the development of the portrait as a real likeness. We have already seen that in the classic periods of Chinese and Japanese art the portrait was, in a sense, considered as a symbol of the social and religious significance of an individual rather than a record of his actual appearance. In the Japan of the thirteenth century this point of view changed toward a more realistic interpretation of the subject, and for reasons not dissimilar from those that brought about this radical innovation in European tradition.

To illustrate the trend in Western art we may select the portrait of Charles VII by the French painter, Jean Fouquet (figure 13), and, as a Japanese counterpart, the likeness of the military tyrant, Minamoto no Yoritomo, painted in the late twelfth century (figure 14). We choose the picture of Charles VII because the subject is a personage known to all as the king crowned by Joan of Arc and because, in the development of the portrait in the West, it occupies a position completely analogous to its Japanese counterpart. The painter of the likeness of Charles VII, Jean Fouquet (1415–1482), was renowned at once as a miniaturist and a painter of portraits. His style, which we shall presently analyze, was a compromise in the assimilation of the fascinating microscopic effects of Flemish portraiture and the more generalized ideal of the Italian Quattrocento. Fouquet lived in the twilight of the age of chivalry. Something of that age still survived in the gorgeous tournaments, the rainbow colors of court dress, and the fairyland castles of the French nobility that were a background for the conceits and artifices of the last of the chivalric poets and an inspiration for its artists. The sensuous and hectic tenor of life and the passion and artificiality of courtly verse paralleled expression in art that at the same time answered the demand of the age for the revelation of everything in earth and heaven, even the most abstract concepts, in real and tangible terms. If Fouquet was in every sense a realistic artist, it is not only because he was exposed to the most advanced experiments toward naturalistic representation in Flemish and Italian painting, but also because he lived in a period of brilliance and misery, unrest and strife, and above all a time of creative change. In contrast to the sensuous frivolity and richness of his own miniature painting, Fouquet's portraiture has a solemnity and gravity no less expressive of his time. Although

14. *Minamoto no Yoritomo*

13. *Charles VII of France*

Fouquet was well acquainted with the work of Flemish and Italian masters of the early fifteenth century, the portraits which he executed for Charles VII reveal certain qualities which were distinctly French and quite distinct from both the Italian and Flemish portrait. One of these traits is certainly present in the intense psychological interest in the sitter, revealed at once in his countenance and in the accessories enframing him. Fouquet's sitters are given a certain elegance and refinement, which are different both from the magic realism of Flanders and the generalized approach of Italian artists. The Flemish portrait in a way engulfs the beholder in the fascinated perusal of the countless minutiae of form and texture that collectively produce the idea of reality. Italian portraits of this same period have a certain icy remoteness and nobility which, in a way, repel the beholder. The subjects of Fouquet's portraits are both accessible to us and yet keep their distance. They have an indescribable suggestion of poise and hauteur in bearing which confers an aristocracy of a different kind. The effect is both precise and calculated, with something of the instinctive grasp of essential facts by the French intellect.

Fouquet's portrait of Charles VII was probably done shortly after 1450, when the king, finally roused from the apathy that allowed him to remain unmoved at the execution of Joan of Arc and the miseries of a land in anarchy, had instituted a new and practical policy, economic and military, which led to the establishment of a France united and great. Only after the conquest of Guyenne in 1450 could he have been described as he is on the frame, *très victorieux*. The portrait of Charles VII is not a state portrait in the usual sense of that term, since the formula is hardly different from that used by Fouquet and his contemporaries for the portrayal of commoners. This type of portrait was so new at the time that formal distinctions had not yet developed for the representation of kings and exalted personages. The principal innovation, of course, resides in the change from the profile portrait to a three-quarters view. This is, in itself, a step from the conceptual and universal type to a more apprehensible and real presentation of a man as we might actually see him. If the king in Fouquet's portrait is not a commanding figure, it is because this suspicious and incalculable man was not a powerful person in reality. Only an effigy in the older tradition could have made him a symbol of kingship. Fouquet has painted him as he saw him in a style of precise linear definition, reinforced with a subdued plastic modeling. If the portrait is less generalized and idealized than an Italian picture, it is because Fouquet as a Northern artist was primarily more concerned with the particular than the ideal aspects of the sitter. Fouquet was certainly aware of the sly intelligence of his subject and the pathos of Charles's not very attractive face, but he has conferred a certain nobility to the mask by the very crispness of his line drawing and the smooth sculpturesque character of the modeling. The flatly abstract curtains of the box and the heavy, voluminous folds of the king's robe set off the very realistic definition of the pinched features.

In this portrait of Charles VII Fouquet was completely the master of the limited spatial problem he assayed. The presence of the fringed valence and parted drapery makes the figure recede into its simple and cell-like space, an interior closed behind the figure by the curtain at the rear of the church box. The cushion at the bottom of the panel was a device which, like the balustrade or window sill used by many of Fouquet's contemporaries as a base for their portraits, at once separates and unites the space of the subject and the space of the beholder. These same elements of the enframement set off the portrait of the king as an isolated figure of majesty.

Fouquet's figures, composed in round and smooth forms, appear almost as paintings of polychromed statues. It is, perhaps, not too much to suppose that the carving of human forms by Renaissance sculptors in rounded, interlocking planes with an elimination of all surface detail that might detract from the evocation of pure solid volume may have suggested to a painter like Fouquet the means for achieving a like clarity and suggestion of three-dimensional form in painting. In this respect, the artist's style seems like a reappearance of the weightiness and serenity of Gothic sculpture joined to the feeling for the beauty of abstract solid volumes in the painting of fifteenth-century Italy. In the present portrait there is an internal architectonic order in the harmony of the abstract shapes that comprise the form: the rounded oval of the cushion supporting the cubic mass of the body and the spheroidal volumes of the head and bonnet.

The parallel of the portrait by Fouquet with the Japanese likeness of Minamoto is striking not only because both reveal a turn to realistic interpretation in their respective traditions, but also because of the psychological interpretation of the subject and the formal means employed for this end. The portrait of Minamoto was one of a series of likenesses of both secular and ecclesiastical personages installed at Jingōji at Kyōto in the twelfth century. Tradition ascribes them to the court artist, Fujiwara no Takanobu (1142–1205). The subject of our portrait, Minamoto no Yoritomo, was a great military leader who, after final victory over the supporters of the imperial throne, founded a military dictatorship at Kamakura. The institution of his Shogunate marked the end of the imperial power in Japan. Thereafter, until the Meiji restoration of 1868, the Emperor lived a cloistered and shadowy existence in Kyōto, a symbol of ancient prestige rather than an active political power. Minamoto's supremacy also terminated the chivalric period of Japanese history, the brilliant and artificial culture of the Fujiwara (983–1185) that is, in a sense, the equivalent of the brilliant sunset of Gothic art in France. This Japanese portrait belongs to a period that in many respects is analogous to the Renaissance in the West. In the Kamakura Period (1185–1392) practicality and emphasis on personal achievement usher in a realism that supplants the artificial elegance and abstract beauty of the earlier portrait art. This was an age when the hard-won victory of a knightly military class brought a new practical authority to Japan. At the same time the austere philosophical discipline of Zen Buddhism, entirely suited to the commonsense needs of the military clan, was challenging the older sects that offered only ritual and prayer. Zen Buddhism, with its emphasis on the individual's working out of his relationship to himself and to the world by meditation and disciplined action was, in a sense, comparable to the teaching of St. Francis in the West. In its emphasis on the validity of every slightest facet of nature as a revelation of the divine, Zen Buddhism, like its Franciscan counterpart, gave a new impetus to realistic rather than completely abstract representation.

In the history of Japanese art there is nothing new about the style of the Minamoto portrait, any more than the actual technique of the portrait by Fouquet marks a radical change from earlier tradition. The novelty is in the employment for realistic ends of a style dedicated for centuries to the abstract ideals of Buddhist art.

The style of this portrait is described by the term, *Yamato-e* (Yamato picture). The Yamato district is traditionally regarded as the original center of Japanese culture, so that the term, Yamato-e, came to be used to define a style which is regarded as distinctly Japanese in mode and taste. As we know it in the Buddhist and secular paintings of Fujiwara times, this is a style of extreme decorative elegance, in which the pictorial elements are reduced to flat, patternized shapes, wrought in exquisite mineral colors and designs in gold and silver leaf. The over-all definition of this style also includes a very expressive type of drawing, sometimes in lines of wiry thinness, sometimes in strokes alternately thinning and thickening, that are more reminiscent of Chinese painting. Typical of the Yamato style in the Minamoto portrait is the sharp, angular silhouette of the black robe that frames an essentially flat area, in which the design of the textile itself, black on black, is conceptually spread out regardless of the foreshortening of the folds. The very austerity of the presentation, both from the point of view of color and arrangement, is typical of the sobriety and direct-ness of Kamakura art. In the hands of a Kamakura artist the Yamato-e style takes on a new force that is far removed from the butterfly gaiety of the earlier Fujiwara manner. The execution of the actual face of Minamoto is done entirely in line and flat tone. It is evident at once that these thin, wiry lines describe the stern ascetic countenance of a real individual. For all the formality of his presentation, Minamoto appears as a distinct personality and not as an effigy. The very stiffness and abstraction of the ceremonial robe accentuate the realism of the cruelly determined face. The attributes of power, the sword and sceptre, are scarcely necessary to reinforce the commanding presence that the artist evokes. Obviously, the isolation of the figure against a blank background marks the persistence of an older type of Oriental portraiture discussed in Chapter One (5). Here, the very austerity of the setting, which consists only of the raised mat of Minamoto's throne, in itself stresses the lean, severe character of the sitter and emphasizes the portrait as a symbol of a military ruler. Like the portrait of Charles VII that for centuries hung in the Sainte Chapelle of Saint Denis, the Minamoto portrait at Jingōji was an icon of temporal power. Its sacrosanct character dictated the idol-like formality of the presenta-tion.

C. THE RELIGIOUS IMAGE

8. *Christ and Buddha*

The simplest type of parallel between works of European and Oriental origin is one of which the examples can be proved to spring from common iconographic and stylistic prototypes. An interesting case in point is the similarity between the earliest representations of the Buddha in India and the first portrayals of Christ in Early Christian art.[1]

The examples chosen for comparison are a marble sarcophagus re-lief of Christ found at Psamatia near Constantinople (figure 15) and a stucco image of Buddha from Hadda in Afghanistan (figure 16). Each may be dated in the fourth century A.D. The figures are both

[1] For a more lengthy exposition of this comparison, see my article, "Gandhāra and Early Christian Art: Buddha Palliatus," *American Journal of Archaeology*, vol. XLIX (1945), no. 4, pp. 445–448.

dressed in a garment derived from the classical *pallium*, a robe in which the right arm appears muffled as though in a sling. The heads of Christ and Buddha have a rather effeminate adolescent face and long, wavy locks of hair. The explanation for this striking resemblance affords an opportunity of demonstrating how parallels like this can arise without the necessity of assuming an influence of one of the examples on the other.

As for the costume, the pallium was not a prevailing fashion of dress when our statues were made, but the association of this robe with ancient representations of philosophers and teachers led to its adaptation for the early images of Christ and Buddha. The resemblance between these first statues of Christ and Buddha is not at all surprising if we consider that both are the result of closely parallel philosophic concepts in the religious complex of the Graeco-Roman orbit. The church fathers refer to Christ as in the line of the great classical teachers; Christ the Pedagogue is thought of as replacing the teachers of the ancients, so that it must have seemed appropriate to early Christian sculptors to represent Him in the dress of the teacher of the classical world.[1] In a similar way, Buddha was regarded as a great teacher whose doctrine replaced the old order, so that the provincial Roman workmen who fashioned his images in Gandhāra chose the classic orator type as the most suitable for portraying the Teacher of the Eastern world.

The early Christian representations of Christ as a young man with long hair appear to be taken over from an earlier Apollo type, like the famous Apollo Belvedere.[2] The texts of early Christianity are filled with passages likening Christ's Resurrection to the sun's rising, His Descent into Hell to the sun's setting. These and other allegorical references to the luciferous character of Christ must have suggested the pagan images of the sun god as appropriate models for representing Him. Owing to the frequent allusions in early Buddhist texts to Buddha's solar character, a similar choice of the classic Apollo type may naturally have suggested itself to the Eurasian artisans who carved the Buddha images of Gandhāra.[3]

The stylistic resemblance between these early figures of Christ and Buddha is to be explained by the fact that, just as sculptors of early Christian images received their training in the Roman workshops of

[1] Cf. the statue of Sophocles in the Lateran Museum, in G. M. A. Richter, *The Sculpture and Sculptors of the Greeks* (New Haven: Yale University Press, 1930), fig. 249.

[2] Cf. A. W. Lawrence, *Classical Sculpture* (London: Jonathan Cape, 1929), plate 130b.

[3] Cf. B. Rowland, *The Art and Architecture of India* (London: Penguin Books Ltd., 1953), plate 32.

15. *Statue of Christ*   16. *Statue of Buddha*

the third and fourth centuries A.D., the carvers of Buddha images in northwest India and Afghanistan—the ancient Gandhāra—were for the most part journeymen sculptors from the Roman Near East. The rather crude and hard appearance of these statues in comparison with what we think of as classic sculpture may be because of the fact that both early Christian and Gandhāra sculpture belong to a period when the Hellenic ideal and the perfection of technique of the Great Age were gradually being replaced by a more abstract, Oriental mode of representation. Also, the earlier technical mastery of the craft was fast disappearing in these centuries of the Roman Empire's disintegration, so that the faces of Christ and Buddha, although resembling the Apollo Belvedere, have a more masklike, dry, and formal quality; in exactly the same way, their garments are represented in terms of lines or sharp ridges instead of the classic naturalistic treatment of the robe as a weighty, voluminous substance.

9. *The Smiling Angels*

It was not long after French archaeologists began the excavation of the ruined Buddhist monasteries at Hadda in southern Afghanistan that a similarity was noted between many of the beautiful stucco heads of deities, priests, soldiers, and kings, and the heads of French Gothic statues of the twelfth and thirteenth centuries. The sculpture at Hadda may all be dated between the third and fifth centuries A.D., when the establishment was reduced to ruin by an invasion of the White Huns. In many cases the comparisons seemed to indicate a truly remarkable anticipation of the spirit and form of Gothic art nearly a thousand years before its appearance in the West. As the examples we have selected for analysis will reveal, this is a kind of parallel that can be explained by the combination of similar backgrounds of technical tradition and spiritual needs, resulting in the emergence of a strikingly similar artistic expression, regardless of the wide separation in geography and time.

The first comparison (figures 15 and 16) of an early Christian relief and a Gandhāra Buddha showed that classical influence in the form of Roman technique and iconography reached northwestern India and Afghanistan as early as the second or third century A.D., where it combined with concepts of native origin to produce an Indian provincial offshoot of Roman Imperial art. In the course of the next centuries the sculptural style of this region underwent a change that may be described as a departure from the ideality and perfect serenity that we think of in connection with Greek and Roman sculpture. This change was in the direction of an interest in inner emotion

18. *Head of Devatā*

17. *Smiling Angel*

in the faces of both deities and mortals, as revealed in their expressions of passion and tenderness, often a kind of wistful pathos. This new suggestion of spiritual feelings and tensions that demanded a peculiarly expressive realism for their presentation is exactly the same quality that distinguishes Roman sculpture of the third and fourth centuries, particularly in the adaptation of the Roman technique by barbarian peoples on the outermost fringes of the Empire. This is a way of looking at the world that reflects a society which was more interested in the individual human being, the tragedy of his fate and the hope of his salvation, than in the calm perfection and frozen beauty of the Olympians. In Roman provincial art this tendency is a reflection of the stirrings toward spiritual awareness on the part of many peoples under the influence of the mystery religions of Asiatic origin that spread the worship of Mithra from the Euphrates to the Rhine. It betokens a concern for the sufferings and emotions of ordinary men, as illustrated by the agonized heads of dying warriors on battle reliefs of the third century and later—a reflection of the universal convulsion that was shaking the entire Roman world.

The head in the collection of the Boston Museum of Fine Arts, probably that of a *devatā* or demigoddess from a large relief composition, is the Indian reflection of the same trend (figure 18). It is an example of classical or Roman style in the East quite different from the Buddha image discussed in Chapter One (8). The striking animation of the features in such marked contrast to the passive serenity of the conventional Buddha head is an Indian illustration of the sculptor's striving for dynamic expression of feeling. The humanity of this head and so many others like it from Hadda and northwestern India is a reflection of late classical art, before the requirements of the new mystical sects of Buddhism had replaced the moral doctrine of action of the early religion by the idea of worship paid to an eternal, divine Buddha, not a mortal teacher, and the possibility of the individual's salvation and rebirth in Paradise.

The famous head of the Smiling Angel of Reims (figure 17), to which the Indian stucco bears such a marked resemblance, is the product of somewhat similar material and spiritual forces. It belongs to a moment in the development of European church art when the reliance on symbol and form, calculated to reveal the nature of an invisible absolute, was being replaced by a style that presented the idea of divinity in more human and readily apprehensible form. The quality of sweetness and wistful tenderness that irradiates the face of the angel is a reflection of that light of a new religion that shines in the words of the thirteenth-century mystics, St. Francis, and the troubadours who extolled the Madonna and all the beings of the sacred hierarchy as intercessors, completely human embodiments of compassion, and immanently accessible.

The figure of Christ analyzed in Chapter One (8) belongs to a style of art that is a complete illustration of the literal objective character of medieval theology with its insistence on the implicit acceptance of the purely intellectual and abstract ideas of divinity. In the Gothic world of the thirteenth century various forces, like the preaching of St. Francis and the gradual disintegration of the power of the monastic orders, inevitably produced an art which was more a reflection of popular thought than of ecclesiastical authority. It was a reflection of the idea inherent in scholastic doctrine that the world is a revelation of God, so that its every detail is worthy of representation as an acceptable reflection of the divine. Beauty of proportion and harmony in a material image is a guide to the apprehension of the final perfection of God. Accordingly, in Gothic sculpture figures and faces appear to be based on human physical beauty and to display a new intensity of feeling both in gesture and expression that was unknown and inappropriate for the hieratic art of earlier centuries. These are human beings conceived as individuals and not as symbols of a humanity distinguished only as the saved and the damned.

In the period when the angel at Reims was carved, sculptors were looking about them at fragments of Roman sculpture which they used as textbooks to achieve a convincing representation of the reality they sought. There is, in other words, a classical background for this Gothic head, just as there is for the Indian example. Furthermore, the angel of Reims displays what appears to be a facial mask drawn perhaps from an actual model. Its anatomy, however, is not an end in itself; it is not even a very convincing representation of the structure of a real face. Its realism, based on observation, is a means to the expression of the divine joy and ecstasy shining in the features of the celestial messenger. The face is composed of only a few very simple planes, the kind of rarefied perfection that we might describe as aristocratic and, hence, in the simple mind of the carver who conceived it, appropriate to expressing by association the heavenly aristocracy of the archangel. As in the devatā of the third century, certain mannerisms like the tilt of the head, the slanting eyes, and the slow curving smile combine to produce an intensified expression of melting tenderness and exquisite joy.

From the point of view of anatomical correctness, neither the Boston head nor the other examples of "Gothic" sculpture from Hadda are any more realistic than the famous Gabriel at Reims. Although there is a classic framework in the description of the hair in wavy incisions and the representation of the face in a few simple planes, the animation of the mask through such devices as the parted lips and softly modeled cheeks is what primarily interested the sculptor. Perhaps the most Oriental feature of this head is the use of a mould for the upper portion of the face that gives a rather dry and formalized look to the eyes and brows, in contrast to the vivacity and freshness of the mouth and chin.

What might appear as an obvious sentimentality, an over-simplification of the features and expressions of the Angel of Reims, is in reality an example of the same desire for clarity and immediately apprehensible order that informed the plan and fabric of the entire cathedral.

It is well to mention in our consideration of these works of art that as we see them out of context, as tiny isolated particles of vast ensembles, they take on an aesthetic significance that was a relatively minor aspect of their original function to instruct and move the beholder to thoughts of the divine. The aesthetic factor—the appealing beauty of the Angel's head—had its importance for what the Abbot Suger implied in his poem on the golden door of his church of Saint Denis: "The dull mind rises to truth through that which is material."

10. St. Demetrius and the Knights

The striking similarities between examples of Oriental and Western art are, in certain cases, to be explained by their development from a common artistic tradition that has been adapted to meet the aesthetic requirements of societies widely separated geographically. A case in point is the close stylistic resemblance between the sixth-century Buddhist wall-paintings of Central Asia and the almost contemporary mosaics of the Byzantine world. In certain respects the wall-painting of Knights from Kizil (figure 20) and the mosaic from the Church of St. Demetrius in Salonika (figure 19) are so similar that it might be possible to mistake them as works of the same school.

The mosaic of St. Demetrius is a perfect example of Byzantine art. It is an illustration of the disappearance of the realistic ideals of classical art in favor of, properly speaking, a stylized, even abstract, conception of the human figure and its surroundings. It is not difficult to see that in this composition the figures have become phantom-like patterns, and the space in which they are placed is as unreal and ambiguous as the forms of St. Demetrius and his companions. There are a number

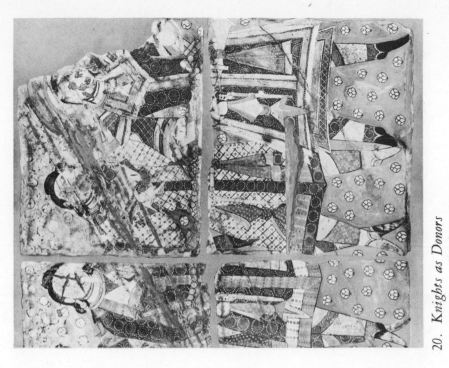

20. *Knights as Donors*

19. *St. Demetrius with Bishop and Subprefect*

of reasons for the emergence of this type of art in the centuries following the fall of the Western Empire. A partial explanation might be
found in the gradual loss of technical competence with the break-up
of the Roman Empire and the consequent disappearance of both patron-
age and the workshop tradition. It could be argued that after the fourth
century, patrons, both secular and religious, had to accept this more
conventionalized art, because, with the loss of the ability to work in
the old tradition of Graeco-Roman times, this was the only style
in which artists could express themselves. There is another factor to
be considered, however, and that is the intrusion into the West of age-
old Oriental or Near Eastern conventions, such as the conception of
the body more as a symbol than an organic structure, the tendency
toward frontality, and the reduction of accessories such as drapery to
a linear pattern entirely in harmony with the unrealistic conception of
the image as a whole.[1] The fact remains that this art, resulting from the
substitution of Oriental hieratic standards for the old humanistic style,
was not only accepted, but encouraged as extremely appropriate for
expressing the changed ideals of Christianity and the empire. By its
very abstraction of form it not only persuaded the beholder of the unreality of divine beings, but was also eminently suitable for portraying
the frozen grandeur of the emperor as a simulacrum of divine rule on
earth. It is not difficult to see that it was, in a sense, the only style
compatible with the Byzantine theocracy, in which imperial power
itself depended upon the ritual enactment on earth of the order and
hierarchy of heaven.

In the mosaic at Salonika the figures of St. Demetrius and his companions are represented standing motionless in frontal position. Their
feet point downward as though they were levitated in air, but this
ambiguity is to be explained by the fact that the ground plane has
disappeared and has merged with the background in a total disintegration of visual space. There is not the slightest suggestion of plastic form
in the bodies which exist only as moving patterns of lines and textile
design. There is an illusion only of a completely unsubstantial and
ghostly form behind the flat drapery. The heads, particularly the faces
of the donors, display an extraordinary asceticism and spiritual vitality. They seem to retain something of that abstract disembodied intensity in portraiture that was so notable a feature of late Roman art. Only

---

[1] It may be added that the medium of mosaic itself contributes to the effect of
unreality. In mosaic the picture is produced by cementing together many small
pieces or cubes of stone or glass. The very nature of this technique imposes a
formalized, abstract execution upon the artist.

here in the faces is there some suggestion of plasticity through the introduction of violent highlights, but even this chiaroscuro is an abstraction which reflects no possible conditions of lighting in the real world. This is a style in which the elimination of all suggestion of actuality is intended to present the principal objects the more forcefully by their reduction to bold, legible patterns of poster-like clarity.

This same insistence on form as a disintegration of substance and the reduction of all pictorial elements to pattern is illustrated even more strikingly by the wall painting of knights from the site of Kizil in Central Asia. This wall painting of the sixth century A.D. is the product of a somewhat similar artistic background to that of the mosaic at Salonika. Here is a style of almost heraldic simplification; the figures have the flatness and insubstantiality of the royal family of playing cards. This wall painting in a Buddhist cave sanctuary represents a group of royal donors. The style of the picture, like that of Byzantine art, is a mixture of elements of classical and Near Eastern origin. It will be noted that space as a pictorial factor does not exist. Figures, foreground, and background are all parts of a formalized pattern in a single plane. This characteristic is even more emphasized by the way in which the sky, around and behind the figures, is filled with a repeated lotus bud motif, as unreal as the design on a carpet. The figures, like their Byzantine counterparts, appear to be standing on tiptoe, and their existence is noted only in terms of the eccentric silhouettes of their flaring mantles and pointed boots. We are, as in the Salonika mosaic, more conscious of the textile designs than the structure of drapery folds and forms beneath. The only surviving classical element in the representation of these figures is the suggestion of arbitrary shading in the reinforced orange contours of the faces. The frozen rigidity of these forms and the reduction of every element to a textile-like design are here, as in Byzantine art, an inheritance from the Near East, specifically from the Iranian art of the Sasanian Period (226–632). It is not difficult to see how the art of the powerful Sasanian Empire of Iran, situated midway between Byzantium and Central Asia, was inevitably destined to exercise a telling influence on the styles of art in these regions with which the Persians were in contact, both in peace and war, for a period of four centuries. It is to be assumed that, just as this nonrealistic art suited the ideals of Byzantium, so in a similar way it was entirely appropriate for the artistic demands of the various mystical sects of Buddhism that flourished in Central Asia. One should add to this the fact that there was no aesthetic feeling for the human form in Turkestan, any more than there was in

China, and that this patternized style of brilliant decoration must have been entirely acceptable to these peoples of nomadic origin, whose whole tradition lay in the minor arts such as textiles and metalwork and not in any monumental figure style.

11. *Symbols of Divinity*

The comparison of a sixth-century Chinese image of the Bodhisattva Maitreya and a twelfth-century Christ of the Pentecost provides a perfect illustration of a phenomenon often encountered in the study of art history (figures 21 and 22). The approximate similarities of technique and purpose result in a startling approximation in the actual material forms, even though the works of art under consideration were created in widely separated areas and centuries removed in time. Such a comparison is a useful one to demonstrate how in the evolution of an art, certain spiritual needs result in the production of forms appropriate to their expression.

The Chinese relief of the sixth century represents the Bodhisattva Maitreya, the Buddha of the Future, whose coming, in a sense, was as eagerly anticipated by Asiatic millions as the appearance of the Apocalyptic Christ was awaited in the dark centuries of medieval time. The Chinese image (figure 22) is at once the product of elements of style and iconography imported from India and Central Asia, combined with no less recognizable contributions from the indigenous artistic tradition of China. Buddhism and its imagery had been imported into the Far East in the early centuries of the Christian era, and by the fifth century A.D., with the firm establishment of the Indian religion, there was already a wholesale and not very original imitation of either Indian or Central Asian models in the form of rock-cut statues and metal images. The present figure retains some of these borrowings: the cross-legged pose and the throne supported by lions had been fixed in the iconography of the Future Buddha in India as early as the second century A.D. The right hand raised in the gesture of reassurance, the crown, and the robe could be traced to a similar source. Whatever canons for the representation of the human figure and its representation in the round that the Chinese sculptors knew were also of foreign origin. There the resemblances end. The conception of the figure in what can be described as geometric and linear terms has nothing whatever to do with the Indian conception of bodily form. The image has an almost ideographic simplification, in that only the portions of real significance to the devotee—the benign mask of the face and the blessing hand—are modeled in full relief. The rest of the body is so

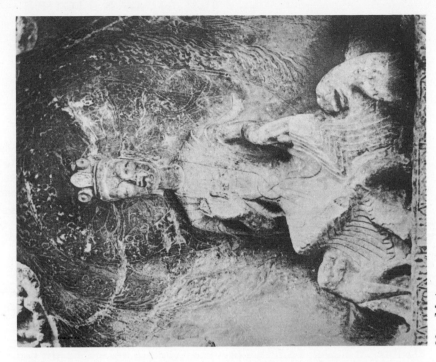

22. *Maitreya*

21. *Christ of the Pentecost*

flattened out that it appears as an immaterial rather than a substantially convincing shape. One is conscious of the form only in terms of the rhythmically repeated curves of the winglike drapery of the skirt and the linear incisions that symbolize scarves and drapery folds on the legs and torso. In none of the earlier and classic periods of Chinese art had there been the development of anything approximating a canon of human beauty such as Indian art had created. In the earliest phases of Chinese civilization the worship of abstract forces of nature and totemic spirits had produced an appropriately abstract expression in terms of zoomorphic forms conceived in intricate and dynamic linear patterns. Partly as an inherent aesthetic trait, partly as a result of the inevitable linear expression inherent in Chinese calligraphy, definition in terms of vitalized linear rhythms implying both design and movement could be recognized as the most characteristic Chinese artistic expression as early as the Han Period (220 B.C.–202 A.D.). When, in the late fifth century, the center of Buddhism in China was moved to the ancient center of Chinese culture at Loyang in Honan Province, a proper Chinese form of Buddhist sculpture developed. The reduction of the image to a relief expressed in calligraphic line rather than in mass certainly reveals the assertion of the Chinese aesthetic standard in its manufacture. At the same time the peculiar feeling of volume by the construction in shapes so abstract as to negate any suggestion of corporeal reality was peculiarly appropriate for expressing the Chinese attitude toward imported Buddhist divinities as strange magical spirits promising all kinds of benefits, spiritual and material, and yet reminiscent of the always abstractly conceived divinities of the indigenous pantheon.

The kinship between the Chinese Buddhist image and its Romanesque counterpart is to be explained up to a point by the fact that both are ultimately derived from a classical—that is, Roman—prototype: the Chinese statue, from the provincial Roman art that flourished in northwest India or Gandhāra;[1] the Christ of Vézelay (figure 21) from the memory of Roman form and technique that endured through all of European medieval art. The Christ of the Pentecost at Vézelay is no more classic in its conception of bodily form than the Chinese statue is Indian or Romano-Indian. The Burgundian Christ is, if anything, more hieratic in the complete rigidity of its folds and its gigantic scale with relation to the other figures in the tympanum. The conception is again an essentially linear one in the definition of the drapery in rhythmically repeated lines that provide an arresting pattern without emphasizing a plastic or material form.

[1] See above Chapter One (8 and 9).

The flamelike lines tend to suggest a floating, spirit-like quality in the towering figure. These surface patterns, these mysteriously dynamic gyres and spirals, communicate an endless, restless movement in a completely ghostly and disembodied shape calculated to express a permanent rather than a transitory reality—not a person or physical presence but rather a ghostly certainty in the hearts of believers, immortal and fixed like a star in the constellation of the heavenly pantheon.

The supernatural canon of anatomy seen in the Romanesque Christ was not evolved on the basis of any human models, but rather on the prototypes afforded by illuminated manuscripts that, since the downfall of the classical Roman tradition, provided the only models for the drawing of figural subjects. The essentially abstract calligraphic idiom of the tradition of illuminated manuscripts occupies the same position in relation to the formation of Romanesque sculpture as the indigenous zoomorphic style of ancient China does to the development of Buddhist sculpture in the fifth and sixth centuries A.D. In both we have a coalescence of certain elements of classic origin, such as the anthropomorphic representation of divinity, and a slight reminiscence of plastic form combined with a completely linear expression. In the West this interpretation stems from the protean form world of medieval penmanship which, in its complexity of design is, like the interlaced pattern of early Chinese bronzes, said to derive from the barbaric ornament of Scythian origin. In both cases whatever classic background of representation in plastic terms lies behind these two images at the opposite ends of the world has been completely subordinated to expression in linear definition, which in its abstract rhythms and movement does not aim to describe real form. Rather it negates form and by the same token contributes to the feeling of immateriality in the statues. In both cases the result is the production of a form different from and superior to human standards and, hence, completely expressive of the supernal and, to men, unknowable nature of the deity. In the Romanesque West, as in sixth-century China, the object of worship was essentially an abstract being incapable of representation, something to be apprehended as a supernatural principle and, hence, very properly to be revealed in symbolical rather than human shape.

12. The Mystic Ideal

Anyone who is familiar with Italian religious painting of the fourteenth century is inevitably reminded of the masterpieces of Buddhist art in medieval Japan. Some authorities have even gone so far as to suggest the possibility of an actual influence of Oriental art on the

23. *The Angel Gabriel. Annunciation (detail)*

24. *Seishi Bosatsu*

painters of Trecento Italy. Certainly in a comparison of the angel from the "Annunciation" (figure 23) painted in 1333 by the Sienese artist, Simone Martini (*ca.* 1285–1344), with a Bodhisattva (figure 24) by an eleventh-century Japanese artist, there are very striking similarities. The discovery of what these resemblances are, and also what differentiates these two examples of religious art, makes such a comparison worthwhile.

Simone Martini belongs to the generation of artists in Italy who first achieved an emancipation from the strict mode of Byzantine tradition and was concerned with an essentially more humanistic presentation of divine beings, both animated and spiritualized, by a new and expressive use of line. He is believed to have been trained by the real founder of the Sienese school, Duccio. Throughout his life he moved among the nobility working for the court of Naples and ending his days in the employ of the exiled papal court at Avignon. The poet, Petrarch, was also numbered among his admiring friends. From the circumstances of his artistic career we may assume that he was exposed to all the most modern ideas of art prevalent in his time: Italian, French, and the lingering vestiges of the Byzantine tradition.

It is not difficult to discern, in studying his angel, that Simone's art is based on a very precise, even hard linear definition. The emphatic contour holds and presents the form to us as a concrete shape set off by the gold background. Here, as in countless other religious paintings of the fourteenth century, the gold leaf indicates an infinite luminous space through the reflections that its metallic surface provides, and at the same time serves as a kind of impenetrable backdrop that restricts the painted forms to the flat planes of the picture. In this respect it approximates the function of the blank background of a Chinese painting on silk or paper. Simone Martini's line, on which the definition of form so largely depends, is not static, but moves in sinuous rhythms that at once animate the form and provide an independent aesthetic attraction of their own. The curvature of the angel's wings and the fluttering tartan might almost remind us of a flourish of Gothic calligraphy. How much this influence of penmanship can be said to persist in the fourteenth century, as it unquestionably did affect the monastic art of the twelfth, is a question difficult to answer. Since Simone Martini was also an illuminator and certainly acquainted with the French style of manuscript painting, it is not too much to suppose that this phase of his art is a kind of exquisite personal refinement of the Northern style.

The conception in terms of dynamic, musically organized linear forms is used by an artist like Simone Martini to impart a flamelike movement to the forms. The suggestion of fluttering in the angel's wings and scarf states that the angelic visitor has just alighted before the Madonna. Again, since the emphasis is so heavily on the skeleton of lines rather than solid form, there is an effectual suggestion of the weightlessness and ghostly quality of the divine being.

In the original painting, the very gorgeousness of the fabrics—the gold and white tunic shadowed with blue, the orange and russet tartan of the mantle, drawn from the sumptuous fashions of contemporary dress—connotes by implication the celestial aristocracy of the archangel. The very refinement of the features, intensely spiritualized and only remotely modeled on an ideal observed in human faces, imparts a feeling of immaculate loveliness which is reinforced by the translucent pallor of the complexion and echoed in the fragility and delicacy of the elongated hands. This idealism of Simone Martini's represents a kind of humanization of the theocratic formulas of the Byzantine tradition in accordance with that confusion of divine and mortal beauty that typifies the chivalric ideal. This manner of presenting a spiritual figure is like Dante's combination of idealism with the poignant recording of individual, naturalistic details; the generalized form of the angel is combined with the meticulous representations of the patterns of the cloth and the exquisite articulation of the olive branch in Gabriel's hand.

Like the icon by Simone Martini, the Japanese painting chosen for comparison represents the exquisite culmination of a great cycle of development in religious art. It typifies a period of esoteric religion in a society ruled by much the same affected code of knightly behavior that characterized the twilight of the Middle Ages in Europe. The painting is a representation of a Bodhisattva, the Buddhist equivalent of an archangel, a being who moved as an emissary from the paradise of the divine Buddha to the world of men. At one time this painting was probably part of a triptych with a representation of the Buddha Amida in the central panel. Amida is the Buddha of Light who presides over the Paradise of the West. His cult, as revealed by the Japanese priest Eishin in the tenth century, enjoyed an enormous popularity in Japan, since the mere invocation of the Holy One's name was guaranteed to insure the devotee a lotus throne in the Blessed Land. The triptych, of which this panel was originally a part, was intended to represent the vision that Eishin saw in the sky over Kyōto. Such banners or screens were placed before the dying, in order to suggest that Amida and his attendants had indeed appeared to receive the soul into Paradise.

In its iconographical trappings and in certain technical aspects the present example is derived from the canons for religious imagery established in India more than half a millennium earlier. We have already seen something of the translation of Indian ideas into the Far East in other examples, so that this process is not entirely unfamiliar. What we have, from the point of view of iconography, is an ultimate Japanese variation on the Indian Bodhisattva type, conceived as a personage dressed in the crown and jewels and trailing skirt of an Indian rajah. Centuries of modification and alterations in accordance with the Chinese tradition lie between the present example and the original. Ultimately of Indian origin, too, is the method of suggesting a kind of arbitrary relief by reinforcing the contour lines with a soft pink shading. There all resemblances to the inherited traditions of the Asiatic mainland ends, and the figure appears as the most typical example of Japanese ideals in Buddhist art. Even in earlier periods Japanese artists had begun to conceive the Buddhist divinities in terms of an exquisitely sensitive and refined feminine ideal, as though by this exaggerated and exquisite fragility revealed in the childlike countenance and flower-like hands it would be possible to express appropriately the ineffable gentleness and purity of the divinity. As can be seen, this is at once a form of humanizing and idealizing that corresponds to the conception of a spiritual being by Simone Martini. Just as the aristocratic refinement of this figure is a kind of reflection of the ideal of feminine beauty that is described for us in the *Tale of Genji*, so the entire character of the painting, although it is a religious painting, is a complete revelation of the rarefied aesthetic culture of the period, no less than Simone Martini's angel is a product of the courtly artificiality of the Trecento. It will be noted in the present painting that, in spite of the retention of the traditional mode of abstract shading, the image is composed largely in terms of line and exquisite surface pattern. The line is of such delicacy that it not only provides a skeleton for the form but imparts to it the same feeling of ghostly insubstantiality that typifies its Gothic counterpart. The lines of the scarves are not only drawn in rhythms of calculated grace, but by their sinuous arrangement suggest the weightless, airy progress of the Bodhisattva's descent. Also worthy of note in this painting is the lotus throne that supports the Bodhisattva. The individual petals are painted in what Chinese painting terminology describes as the *boneless* method, whereby the form is indicated not in terms of line or brushwork but in softly graduated washes of solid color that simultaneously suggest both relief and local tone. The employment of this entirely artificial technique imparts a curious luminosity to the miraculous flower that glows with a strange incandescence against the dark silk.

The parallels between this painting and its European equivalent can be seen to exist primarily in the artist's use of line as an instrument to evoke a spiritual presence in the most ethereal pictorial terms. In both cases, also, the ideal is based in part on a hypersensitive refinement of a human model that by its very unearthly character is calculated to suggest the remote celestial aristocracy. It is an ideal that in both cases is produced by the demands of a mystical religion of salvation and the refinements of an earthly aristocracy.

13. The Baptist and the Sage

What we mean by realism in the treatment of the human figure is either the result of man's interest in himself or the satisfaction of scientific curiosity in artistic terms, and, in portraiture, is the result of a necessity to make a recognizable facsimile of the sitter. In religious art realism appears when all other forms of art are realistic, periods when even invisible concepts have to be cast in a mould of earthly experience in order to persuade the beholder of their validity. Illustrations of this phenomenon can be found in both East and West in many periods. We may choose as an illustration of this parallel development a statue of the Buddhist sage Basu (figure 26) of the Kamakura Period (1185–1392) in Japan and the fifteenth-century Italian sculptor Donatello's statue of St. John the Baptist (figure 25). Both could be described as evocations from the past, not true portraits, but reconstructions in a realistic framework of appropriate likenesses for great historical personages in Buddhist and Christian tradition.

The wooden statue of Basu (Sanskrit, *Vasishtha*) was carved by Tankei, a member of a dynasty of sculptors, who, in the thirteenth century, initiated an extremely realistic manner of representing the members of the Buddhist pantheon and church. The subject is an obscure Indian sage who served the Bodhisattva Avalokiteśvara on Mt. Potalaka in India. In both painted and sculptured *mandalas* or assemblies he is included among the followers of the Bodhisattva of Mercy. Basu is represented as an emaciated old man with a tiger skin wrapped about his loins, with a Buddhist text held out in his left hand, and supporting himself by a cane in his right hand. The statue is carved in a style that seems to approach verism, not only in the differentiation of

25. *St. John the Baptist*   26. *Basu, One of the Attendants of Kwann*

textures in the carving but in the literal recording of every bony protuberance and vein. This naturalism even extended to the insertion of crystal eyes. Realism employed in religious art, of course, has the aim of persuading the beholder to believe in the existence of a saintly person by presenting that person in terms of everyday experience. Such an approach may, as in certain examples of Spanish Baroque art, lead to a negation of the religious nature of what is represented. In this statue of Basu, however, there is such a suggestion of concentration, as though the eyes were fixed on some invisible presence, that the image assumes a strangely moving spiritual character, completely transcending the tour de force of its naturalistic technique. In spite of its seeming realism, the face has something of the symbolic abstract forcefulness of a mask in the way that the patterned lines of the wrinkles framing the eyes and mouth enhance the intensity of vision suggested by the deep-sunk eyes and the tremulous parting of the lips that seem about to speak. There is almost an informality in the moving immediacy of the pose, in the way in which the stoop of the shoulders and the bend in the knee suggest a momentary pause in the faltering gait. This is a style that was, perhaps, inevitable for a practical, materialistic age which demanded the translation of even the most esoteric concepts of Buddhism into tangible shapes of reality.

Although Donatello's selection of the wasted form of St. John as a subject for his chisel might be regarded as a forecast of the nineteenth-century penchant for subjects that would provide a pretext for a tour de force in the suggestion of surface texture and the pathos of decrepitude, there are indications that the great Florentine had quite different reasons for expression in this extreme of realistic definition. An emaciated figure, like a superhuman attenuated one, automatically signifies the idea of asceticism and a suppression of the physical aspects of the body. For Donatello the selection of this wiry, spare ideal of masculine beauty must have seemed a peculiarly appropriate one for expressing his conception of the spiritual virility of the Baptist. The realism of the statue in no way approaches the veristic definition of its Japanese counterpart. It consists in the accuracy of anatomical proportion and articulation with a suggestion of a textural differentiation in the contrast between the appropriately rough surface of the hairy garment and the smoothness of the marble flesh. The face itself, like all of Donatello's embodiments of the ghostly heroes of Christendom, is, in no sense, a mere factual recording of a model. The slight elongation of the mask, the emphasizing of the sunken cheeks, and the wryly expressive mouth combine with the suggestion of translucent pallor in the surface of the marble to produce the effect of an inner spiritual presence that seems to speak through the mask of stone. In a manner somewhat analagous to that of the Japanese statue, the suggestion of momentarily arrested movement in the pose and the nervous tension of the hands contribute at once to the spirituality and immediacy of the realization.

We have an illustration in both cases of how realism is used, not for its own sake, but for the more intense embodiment of spiritual ideals. In each case the artist strove for the revelation of an inner ghostly presence in a framework of naturalistic perception. It was precisely the realistic evocation of that presence that made it entirely under-standable to all in the only terms that could be understood in periods when belief was no longer implicit but had to be induced.

Chapter Two

Landscape

W<small>E ARE</small> surrounded with things we have not made and which have a life and structure different from our own: trees, flowers, grasses, rivers, hills, clouds. For centuries they have inspired us with curiosity and awe. They have been objects of delight. We have recreated them in our imagination to reflect our moods. And we have come to think them as contributing to the idea which we call nature. Landscape painting marks the stages in our conception of nature." In these words of Kenneth Clark,[1] we have as nearly complete a definition of landscape painting and its function as one could hope to find. In East and West landscape has always been a pictorial record of man's communion with nature. Whether we turn to the writings of John Constable or the Sung painter, Kuo Hsi, we find the expression of the idea that landscape painting, like nature herself, provides a solace and retreat in solitude and grandeur and infinite space. While landscape painting has the capacity of soothing the spirit through its arranged prospect of quiet and order, this is only

[1] *Landscape into Art* (London: J. Murray, 1949), p. 1.

one of its functions. Heroic or tragic landscape in the Orient and Europe is concerned with producing our heightened awareness of the vast and terrible in nature, the endless change and flux of man's environment, expressed in terms of mountain and cataract, mist and storm, and the dynamic elements of light and space.

In the Orient, landscape paintings have been the pictorial statement of the age-old Chinese regard for nature as an escape from the machine of society, an escape from human emotions into a world of refinement and grace and quiet: Chinese connoisseurs liked to lose themselves in wandering in the painted distances of a landscape scroll. It is for this reason that the Chinese landscapists strove for interpretations of mood and spirit, rather than the rendering of the visual and plastic effects sought after by their Western counterparts.

From the most remote periods, the Chinese have literally been in love with nature. This was a romantic ardor, pagan and mystical, that grew out of the age-old ritual worship of the powers of heaven and earth, the attribution of divinity to the five great mountains. In times of national anarchy the wilderness became the only retreat for scholars and poets; so it is not surprising that, from the earliest times, the Chinese humanists sought and found an absorption in nature that at times amounted to an almost religious fervor for wild places. The cultivation of this idea of retreat into nature in search of a revelation of the all-pervading forces and spirit of the universe had from early times been a part of the religion of Taoism. The whole of the Chinese point of view toward nature and its recording in painting is epitomized for us in the words of the Sung painter, Kuo Hsi, who wrote:

Why does a virtuous man take delight in landscapes? It is for these reasons: that in a rustic retreat he may nourish his nature; that amid the carefree play of streams and rocks, he may take delight; that he may constantly meet in the country fishermen, woodcutters, and hermits, and see the soaring of the cranes, and hear the crying of the monkeys. The din of the dusty world and the locked-in-ness of human habitations are what human nature habitually abhors; while, on the contrary, haze, mist, and the haunting spirits of the mountains are what human nature seeks, and yet can rarely find.[1]

This is only the Chinese equivalent of Emerson's lines from "Waldeinsamkeit":

> Cities of mortals woe-begone
> Fantastic care derides
> But in the serious landscape lone
> Stern benefit abides.

[1] *An Essay on Landscape Painting*, trans. Shio Sakanishi ("Wisdom of the East Series" [London: J. Murray, 1936]), p. 30.

Often, the Chinese point of view presents a prophecy of the ideas of the romantics of Goethe's generation—that landscape should be a kind of veil through which one may glimpse a loftier reality.

As we are already aware from our examination of figure painting, Chinese artists place a great deal of emphasis on the quality of inspiration conceived as a kind of superhuman outside force that transforms the painter and fills him with creative energy. The painter, Wang Wei, said that the clouds, peaks, and cliffs should be formed as by the power of heaven; then, if the brushwork is free and bold, the picture will be penetrated by the creative power of nature. A critic relates that Wang Wei

conceived the thing in his mind; his hand responded, and it was done as conceived. This was because creative activity resided in the spiritual part of his nature and because he grasped to a high degree the inspiration of heaven [1] . . . His cloudy peaks and rocks were superior to nature . . . by his free manner of painting he becomes one with the creative power of nature.[2]

In other words, his pictures were creations based on nature and their forms appeared possessed of a dynamic life of their own.

Great Chinese landscapes illustrate the first of the Six Principles of Chinese painting, the idea of presenting the spirit or breath of things as revealed in the specific movement and life that vitalizes them in accordance with natural laws. This means that a painting of mountains must make us aware of the essential architecture of their growth in terms of stability as well as structure and a suggestion of their appropriate weightiness and mass. We should be able to feel their summits towering into the vastness of the sky and their foothills as massive roots anchored in the earth. Again, it is better to paint a distorted tree that seems to grow than a naturalistic one that is dead and lifeless as a photograph; better to paint a wave that seems eternally to curve and break than a frozen record of momentary light reflected on the surface of a single billow.

The immortalization of the grandeur of the natural furniture of the world, which, in China, amounts to a kind of lyric and mystical aestheticism, finds its only true equivalent in the romantic period of Europe. In the Western world what we might describe as the humanistic bias and the Greek worship of personal deities has militated against the growth of a real feeling for our natural home: whereas, in Greece, a

[1] O. Sirén, *The Chinese on the Art of Painting* (Peiping: H. Vetch, 1936), p. 63.
[2] *Ibid.*, p. 145.

dryad or a wood nymph personified a grove or tree, it was the grove
or tree itself that in China was regarded as a divine manifestation of
the workings of the universal spirit. In the darkling centuries of the
medieval period the Greek wood gods were transformed into the demons who plagued the holy men who had retired to the woods or the
desert in order to test their powers of resistance against the Evil One.
The result was that for more than a thousand years the wilderness became a kind of symbol of the sinful and unholy. Then, too, the dangers
that beset the traveler in wild and desolate regions did not make for
the growth of either a religious or a poetic feeling toward nature. It
was only in the seventeenth century, when the demons and the dangers
were cleared out from the underbrush, that there began a serious and
philosophic speculation about nature and a poetic and artistic interpretation of her moods. One could say that, beginning with the work of
the great seventeenth-century landscapists, Poussin, Claude and Salvator
Rosa, the pictorial and poetic interpretation of landscape in the West
divides itself into classic and romantic types of expression. The classic
landscapists of the seventeenth century might be said to reorder and
improve nature, to paint her as she might have been if at liberty to express her moods and shapes freely and perfectly, while the romantic
painter and poet were more interested in the wild and fierce aspects
of nature or in nature as a revelation of the awesome mystery of the
divine.

1. *Seasonal Panoramas*

The beginnings of landscape painting both in the East and West are
characterized by an allegorical representation of a natural scene, a point
of view that is, of course, quite different from painting nature for its
own sake. The necessity of including certain recognizable elements,
even within this limited framework of approach, was a step toward
the painting of unified landscape based on actuality in detail and general articulation. Because it is a reflection of this point of view, the
countryside which appears in Ambrogio Lorenzetti's (*d.* 1348) "Good
Government in the Country" (figure 27) is so akin to the landscapes
typifying the four seasons, painted in China in the eleventh century
(figure 28). In both, the presentation is essentially a conceptual one,
in which hills and mountains are conelike eminences covered with trees
and shrubs that are generalized ideographs rather than realistic recordings of any particular species. Just as the Chinese wall painting is filled
with deer typifying the winter season, the Lorenzetti fresco is populated by a host of little figures illustrating peaceful life in the country-

28. *Winter Landscape*

Good Government in the Country

side.[1] The aim of the Italian picture of country life was not a realistic
or even poetic recording of landscape, but rather a didactic illustration of the benefits of security that come from good government in the
country. The Chinese tomb decoration, together with the paintings
on the three other walls of the sepulchre, was intended to symbolize
a season of the year, partly as a decoration, partly as a pictorial emblem of the ever-renewed process of nature even in the world of the
tomb. As part of the age-old system of Chinese cosmology the seasons
of the year had been associated with the points of the compass. In
earlier Chinese tomb paintings and in the designs on ancient mirrors
of bronze and silver, the directions and the seasons were typified by
the shapes of the four beasts associated with the four points of the
compass.[2] It is significant that in the eleventh-century wall paintings it
is an actual scene, a kind of microcosm of nature that replaces the earlier animal symbolism. In other words, a representation of nature now
typifies the cosmic mysteries of change and direction. It could be said,
in the same way, that Ambrogio Lorenzetti's archaic landscape is a
restatement in terms of nature of what in other parts of the fresco is
implied by the old anthropomorphic symbols of the seasons of the year
and the personification of Justice, Peace, and Fortitude.

In neither of these landscapes is there anything even approximating
a representation of nature as a unified totality. Such a conception was
both beyond the capacity and beyond the aims of the painters. The
Chinese tomb painting gives the impression of a composition that is
made up of many separate details combined to give a complete impression. Although the barren, rounded hills may be ultimately reminiscent
of the Mongolian landscape, they are drawn as a number of separate
conical shapes presented as essentially flat, overlapping silhouettes. The
animated drawings of deer are simply attached to this background,
and the pine trees that fill the foreground, although they reveal a certain feeling for the articulation of actual trees, again appear as details
attached to the backdrop. There is no sense of any systematized spatial
relationship between the various elements that compose the picture, so
that the whole conception may be assigned to an archaic stage in the
development of landscape when the whole was to be apprehended by
the successive recognition of its parts.

[1] The activities of the figures in the Lorenzetti fresco include plowing, sowing,
reaping, and flailing, so that the picture is a composite seasonal landscape embrac-
ing the peasants' work in every part of the year.
[2] These were the Green Dragon (Spring: East), the Red Phoenix (Summer:
South), the White Tiger (Autumn: West), and the "Black Warrior" or Tortoise-
and-Serpent (Winter: North).

Lorenzetti's landscape illustrates an exactly similar moment in the development of landscape painting in the West. It is the first painting of its kind in which there is at least a recognizable similarity to a definite place, although this resemblance is arrived at by an identical conceptual process. The scene is made up of many separate topographical elements that we recognize as familiar in the Tuscan landscape today, but arranged as a kind of generalized panorama without reference to any one specific view. The landscape is composed of many individual domical hillocks and checkerboard fields receding in a succession of overlapping planes to the high horizon. Some of the hills are covered with verdure; others are barren like the volcanic Creti to the east of Siena. The result is a kind of ideographic suggestion of particular natural features characterizing the landscape around the city of Siena in all directions. The many little figures that inhabit this setting are typically occupied in the various activities of plowing, flailing, harvesting, and hunting that are immemorially associated with life in the country. The same thing is true in the Chinese "Winter Landscape" in which the spectator's identification of these many morphologically correct details gives him the impression of looking at a real landscape, although it is composed without any sense of the spatial or atmospheric relationships that one would discern in an actual landscape. It could, perhaps, be said that in both cases this archaic approach, intuitive and symbolic, was appropriate for a representation that had as its chief aim legibility and symbolism. Both of these landscapes in their respective traditions are remarkable in that they show the painter's awareness of actual nature. It required only an integration of the multiple details to produce a unified and poetic interpretation of the theme.

2. In the Forest

At the famous exhibition of Chinese art held at Burlington House in London in 1935, two of the most admired paintings were a pair of hanging scrolls, representing "Deer in a Maple Forest" (figure 30). These pictures are traditionally attributed to the Five Dynasties period (906–960 A.D.). The landscapes invite a comparison with one of the earliest true landscapes in the West—Albrecht Altdorfer's (1480–1538 A.D.) "Landscape with St. George and the Dragon" (figure 29)— not only because both are forest scenes, but because in each we get for the first time an impression of the totality of nature.

These Chinese paintings, when they were first exhibited to Western connoisseurs, were so unlike the accepted ideas on Chinese art that they were generally described as reflecting Western, presumably Persian,

29. *St. George and the Dragon*

30. *Deer in a Maple Forest*

influences. Actually, they are the equivalent in landscape of a type of realistic art that is well-known in the realm of bird-and-flower painting and far earlier landscape traditions. The painting we have chosen for illustration shows a herd of deer in a grove of maples. The animals, which are represented in a great variety of characteristic poses, are painted in a technique of outline and local tone, with a very slight and subtle suggestion of shading to give a feeling of solidity to the individual forms. The maple trees, which are painted in light yellow and variegated shades of neutralized red, at first give the impression of a series of screens overlapping one another in alternate patches of light and dark colors. It will be noted that the individual trees, however, are drawn with a definite sense of their articulation and shape. The total effect is not entirely a decorative one, for the very diversity of silhouette pattern and color provides a wonderful illusion of the density of the foliage and the endless extent of the forest interior. This is something quite different from those earlier Chinese landscapes, in which the forms of nature were represented only by symbols with but little suggestion of the actual growth or complication of nature as a whole. Although this type of painting, depending on precision of drawing and delicacy of color, was to disappear in favor of the more abstract and romantic effects obtainable in monochrome ink, this forest landscape represents the same stage in the development of a really organic view of nature as some of the more grandiose mountain landscapes of the same period. What is important, too, is that this is one of the earliest Chinese paintings in which the mood of a season is transcribed in terms of the elements of nature poetically associated with it.

The little painting by Altdorfer of "Landscape with St. George and the Dragon" can serve as a very illuminating comparison with the Chinese painting, because it, too, is representative of one of the earliest awakenings to the fullness and complexity of the natural world. We are struck, of course, by the obvious similarity in the great shield of trees that rises to the top of the little panel, screening all save a tiny view of distant plains and mountains in the lower foreground. There is, as in few other pictures, a feeling of the immensity and fullness of the primeval forest, its solitude and stillness interrupted only by the battle between St. George and his dragon antagonist, a little incident almost lost in this gigantic panorama of verdure. The enormous complexity of the dense growth of trees is clarified as in the Chinese maple forest by the silhouetting of individual light masses of ferns and beech leaves against passages of darker greens at the back. Although in a sense deliberately patternized, the variety and the shapes of these foliate motifs

are such as to give an impression of the tangled disorder and impenetrable density of the forest growth. There is a wonderful suggestion of
the treetops opening in the wind, the leaves turned upward to catch the
reflections of the sunlight. In contrast to earlier European landscapes,
in which nature was ordered into a more or less prearranged stage-set
or represented by the limning of individual details, there is here, for
the first time, an attempt to suggest the uncontrolled growth and com-
pleteness of nature as she really is. The artist's choice of the mysterious
forest setting for the triumph of St. George over the dragon probably
still reflects the old medieval conception of the wilderness as the do-
main of evil and lurking danger. But the very fact that an artist was
able to paint a forest interior as a subject both awesome and beautiful
represents very much the same awareness of nature exhibited by the
Chinese paintings of "Deer in a Maple Forest." The differences lie, of
course, in the more deliberate and essentially abstract patternizing of
the tree forms in the Chinese painting, together with a complete elimination of interest in the irregularities of light and texture that animate
Altdorfer's forest interior.

For the history of painting in China the painting of "Deer in a
Maple Forest" marks the end, rather than the beginning, of a pictorial
tradition. This is as far as the Chinese painter cared to go in a realistic
interpretation of nature. We may gather from surviving examples of
painting and from literary sources as well, that in the Five Dynasties and
Northern Sung periods Chinese artists in every category of painting—
figure, landscape, and still-life—had arrived at a solution for the portrayal of these various aspects of visual reality that suited their aesthetic
needs. The dominant aesthetic need was, as we may see in every
branch of Chinese art, not a precise transcription of nature in the sense
of total visual effect, but rather the representation of the essence or
spirit peculiar to the manifold creations of the world of nature. Once
the technical problems had been solved for the achievement of this de-
sired expression, there was no need to explore further for the artistic
means of presenting a more accurate or scientific recording of the outward appearance of things. Although obviously the kind of academic
realism achieved by artists of the Five Dynasties and Sung periods con-
tinues as a tradition through countless later generations of painters,
there is no change in the direction of greater realism, but only the variations to be expected from different artistic personalities repeating the
same formula. All later innovations in Chinese painting occur in the
exploring of abstract and romantic possibilities of expression in monochrome ink.

The painting by Altdorfer, like the occasional landscapes of Leonardo and Dürer, is one of many small beginnings by Western artists in their concentrated search for the solution to the problem of how to represent in terms of paint the complete visual effect of nature by means of form, color, light, and texture. Altdorfer's "Landscape with St. George and the Dragon" lends itself peculiarly well to comparison with the Chinese painting, not only because it is one of the earliest attempts to suggest the totality of nature, but, like its Chinese counterpart, it belongs to a moment when actual observation and self-imposed convention or pattern were combined with peculiar effectiveness to present the real essence, as well as the form, of the theme.

3. *Demon Groves*

The use of elements from nature to predicate a poetic mood is a tendency that could only make its appearance in essentially romantic periods in the art of East and West: it is partly the result of man's coming to identify his own feelings with the aspects of his surroundings, smiling or sinister, and a response or awakening to the pictorial possibilities of the wild, disordered side of nature, which is the opposite of any academic classical canon of performance. This is a point of view that is first exemplified for us in Chinese painting of the Five Dynasties period (906–960 A.D.), when landscape finally becomes an independent category of expression in the Far East. Our illustration is by the tenth-century artist, Li Ch'êng, a wonderfully moving painting in the Abe Collection entitled "Reading the Tablet" (figure 32). The picture represents a traveler seated on a donkey, scrutinizing with fearful intensity the inscription on a stele that rises like a menhir before a grotesque group of pine trees that arch their dragon branches against the empty sky. These trees are not mere ideographic symbols, but convincing ideations based on the observation of the actual structure of pines. An immediate predecessor of Li Ch'êng's, Ching Hao, describes in a famous essay how he sketched a weird grouping of pine trees and succeeded in "catching their spirit." By this we may assume he meant a recording, not so much of outward appearance, as of the essence of their articulation and growth. It is this very same epitomizing of all that we associate with the grotesque, almost anthropomorphic, shapes of old and stricken trees that characterizes the painting of Li Ch'êng. Indeed, it is the concentration and isolation of the twisted trees with their tortuous, ironhard trunks and crab-claw branches that communicate an almost sinister mood to the painting. Curve and countercurve of branches, almost like the favorite mannerism of the Chippendale style, bestow a feeling of sinuous movement to the strangely animated grove. There is no overstatement. Trees and stele, traveler and donkey, lost in the cold grayness of the picture's twilight tonality, are a unified, quiet comment on the strangeness of a lonely place apart, and on the forgotten history almost overgrown by nature that is the object of the intruder's scrutiny. The composition, arranged with the main pictorial masses placed to the left of center and balanced by the entire emptiness of the righthand portion of the picture, is an early instance of the classic method of asymmetrical balance that we encounter in every category of Chinese art. It might be mentioned, too, that the so-called crab-claw convention of the branches and tree forms demands a definition of each branch and twig with the sharp point of the brush, unerringly tracing the outlines of the consecutive parts of the growth. We note also that the arrangement of this picture consists not of just one, but actually five grouped pines; its disposition with the infinitely tortuous interlacing of the separate trees corresponds very closely to the classic example for painting such a complicated growth of trees that is given in *The Mustard Seed Garden*, the famous seventeenth-century manual of painting.

The blasted tree as a foreground accessory is a familiar shape in the picturesque landscapes of the romantic period. It is there in order to stress the wild and unkempt and even eerie quality of nature. An even more proximate comparison of a natural form used to create a mood in landscape can be found in a detail of the German painter Matthias Grünewald's (1468–1531) panel of the "Temptation of St. Anthony" (figure 31) for the famous Isenheim altarpiece. The composition as a whole represents the saint in the toils of a crawling army of obscene deformities and monsters. The "Temptation of St. Anthony," a subject taken from the life of St. Athanasius, was one dear to the period of Grünewald, in which belief in the omnipresence of the Fiend dominated popular Christian thought. Grünewald was an artist whose history is obscure, but it is known that he was influenced by the mystical visions of St. Bridget and the demonology of the time. In paintings like this, which represents a veritable catalogue of demons, the fantasms were drawn partly from descriptions in the saint's life, partly from the monsters of the bestiary and creatures spawned from the painter's own vivid imagination. In this panel the nightmare is heightened by the way in which all nature, dreadful and deformed, enters into the demoniacal conspiracy against St. Anthony. We need only look at the tree silhouetted against the icy blue of the background. It stretches its dead, moss-covered branches in a kind of malediction

31. *Temptation of St. Anthony* (*detail*)

32. *Reading the Tablet*

above the amphitheatre of monstrosities. Actually, this pine is no more
than a silhouette set against the background of distant mountains. Drawn
with great freedom in long, unbroken strokes of the brush, it has an
extraordinary vibrancy and expressiveness, as a recording of growth
characteristic of a pine in addition to its integral dramatic role in the
setting. The ragged, broken elements of landscape, together with the
ghostly pine, are as important to the mood as the purposely tortuous
drawing in Li Ch'êng, combining with the twilight colors to produce
an atmosphere of spectral unreality exactly appropriate to the character
of the demoniacal struggle. Although a picture like Grünewald's would
be unthinkable for a Chinese artist, who would be horrified at its overstatement and crowding, Grünewald's use of isolated elements of nature as evocative contributions to an over-all mood provides a parallel
to the practice of Oriental artists at a time when painters in the West
were barely aware of nature except as an allegory of the divine.

4. *Man in Nature*

Pen and wash drawings of landscapes by European artists lend themselves to comparisons with Far Eastern landscapes owing to the approximate similarity of the technique to the Chinese use of ink and
wash drawings with the brush. In certain cases such as the present
comparison between Pieter Brueghel's (1525–1560) drawing of an
"Alpine Landscape" (figure 33) and the "Autumn Weather in the
Yellow River Valley" (figure 34) by the eleventh-century Chinese
artist Kuo Hsi, the approximation amounts to a very close spiritual
parallel as well. In no case can this resemblance be explained by anything like an actual influence, but rather through the action of like
spiritual inspiration expressed in similar, but independently evolved
techniques.

Pieter Brueghel, who is remembered chiefly for his interpretation
of humble parables and Biblical themes in terms that are always
strangely lyrical and completely Flemish in their expressive simplicity,
was an artist whose style emerged partially from the surrealist phan-
tasmagoria and diabolical nightmares of Hieronymus Bosch, combined
with an acquaintance with Italian Renaissance art gained in the course
of a youthful journey to Italy. It is always apparent that Brueghel remained completely unaffected by the classical beauty of Italian painting
and its scientific attainments, whereas the towering icy majesty of the
Alps and the golden radiance of the Italian sun remained with him always as powerful creative memories. The present drawing, like the
artist's painting of "Icarus" and the "Winter Landscape" in Vienna is

an imaginative recreation from memory of his youthful vision of Alpine scenery. The drawing is executed in ink outline, reinforced with multiple minute strokes of the pen which, by their repeated shapes and density, suggest the texture of things like rocks and trees and at the same time impart a feeling of plasticity to the component parts of the picture.[1] The enormous impressiveness of the landscape is achieved by the device of raising the summits of the mountains almost to the top of the paper as the last in a series of planes leading the spectator into the composition. Another Brueghel mannerism is the salient foreground from which the spectator feels that he, together with the solitary figures just over the edge of this promontory, will drop into the vast amphitheatre of the plain below that stretches to the foot of the mountain bastion. The diminutive scale of the figures set against the towering magnificence of the landscape creates the impression of puny human beings lost in the enfolding immensity of nature. The suggestion of the vastness of the universe revealed in landscape and the inexorable passing of the seasons, aspects of space and time of which man's activity is only an insignificant part, are the two refrains that are repeated many times in Brueghel's finished panel paintings. This awe in the face of the overwhelming immensity of nature is a factor that very closely relates Brueghel's conception of landscape to the performance of masters in the Far East.

The landscape by Kuo Hsi with its defile of majestic serrated peaks is a translation into pictorial terms of the wildly picturesque mountain scenery of southern and western China. Like the drawing by Brueghel, it is created entirely on the basis of memory. The technique of the painting consists of pale transparent washes of water color to give a slight suggestion of color and relief to the various parts of the painting. This is reinforced by the employment of a limited number of brushstrokes which by their shape and texture are designed to suggest the appearance of specific things in the world of nature. Chinese artists, even as early as the tenth century, began to evolve a fixed vocabulary of brushstrokes that by long experience had been found entirely appropriate to suggest, in a shorthand way, the stratification of rocks, the brittle or pliant structure of trees, the pattern of waves or swaying grasses. This vocabulary of brushstrokes is closely related to Chinese calligraphy, in that strokes, pliant or hard, in lines alternately thickening and thinning, are employed to define the structure of characters or ideographs in Chinese writing. In the landscape by Kuo Hsi it is easy to see how a repetition of angular "hook-and-hack" strokes have been

[1] The traces of bistre wash on the drawing are an addition by a later hand.

33. *Alpine Landscape*

34. *Autumn Weather in the Yellow River Valley*

used to define the rugged stratification of the central peak; and other strokes like raveled hemp fibers are employed to suggest the texture and erosion of the lesser slopes. It will be noted that the artist's repertory includes a specific and appropriate type of brush drawing for the definition of every least detail in the composition. It can be readily seen that this is a method that, through the over-all statement in repeated linear phrases, makes for a formal as well as textural harmony in the whole. A close inspection of this picture by Kuo Hsi will reveal the presence of a number of tiny figures making their way across the shallow foreground. The very minuteness of their scale was a device on the part of the Chinese artist to emphasize the vastness of the mountain panorama, with the implication, too, that man is but a small and insignificant part of the great machine of the universe.

Though there are many similarities between these landscapes from the point of view of general tonality and the distortion of perspective, the treatment of them differs: Brueghel's study is a form drawing without the precise interest in both definition and the enlivening of surface that the Chinese use of brushstrokes provides. There is yet a more fundamental distinction between the two wash drawings. Since, in the Brueghel landscape, the emphasis is on the figures of the peasants who make their way into the vast amphitheatre of mountains that is at once their home and their fate, the drama of nature's immensity is related in human terms. In the Chinese landscape the eternal forms of nature are themselves the enactors of the drama of space and time. In this giant panorama of mountains, mists, and trees the almost imperceptible little figures are completely enfolded. Their role and destination are unimportant; they are wanderers, with whom the spectator may identify himself in exploring the recesses of a landscape, the forms of which, in their suggestion of permanence and immensity, reflect the Chinese idea of nature as the ultimate revelation of the spirit that animates the cosmic machine.

5. *Emotion Recollected*

In contrast to the types of landscape represented by Brueghel and Kuo Hsi, in which forms are defined as solid masses existing in space, we have a different approach to landscape in which the painter is concerned with the color,[1] air, and light surrounding the elements of nature. This is a point of view that can be described as romantic since

[1] In the monochrome pictures chosen for analysis, color, although not actually present, is implied in the variety of gradation and texture in the ink or watercolor wash.

35. *Landscape of the Campagna*

36. *Spring Landscape*

the very indefiniteness of the forms, the suggestion of their merging and emerging in shrouding veils of mist or dissolved in a splendor of light are calculated to evoke the feeling of the mystery of nature, subject to eternal dynamic change, and conceived in terms—color, air, and light—that appeal more to the senses than to the intellect.

The romantic landscape is predominant in China in the work of artists of the Northern Sung period (960–1127), although tradition credits the invention of landscape executed in monochrome atmospheric effects to Wang Wei of the eighth century. In Europe the beginnings of this approach can be seen in the pen and wash drawings or sketches by painters like Guercino and Claude Lorrain although it is not until the nineteenth century that the romantic landscape, properly speaking, makes its appearance in the history of art.

A typical painting by Mi Fu (1051–1107), such as the example in the Palace Museum of Peking (figure 36), lends itself to comparison with a wash drawing (figure 35) by Claude Lorrain (1600–1682) because both are seemingly composed in dense masses of ink and wash, and a feeling of solidity is imparted to the forms by these dark shapes.

Mi Fu's principal method of painting was to build up the conical mountains and foliage in repeated horizontal strokes laid on with the side of the brush. Both a variegation in the value of the ink and the appropriately denser or lighter massing of these fastidious touches of the brush suggest not only the plasticity of things in nature, but their emergence from the screens of mist that hang between the foreground and the background plane. The presence of these clouds and also the very softness and irregularity of the contours of trees and mountains suggest their absorption in the hazy atmosphere in an almost impressionistic way. There is the feeling, as so often in Chinese landscape, that all things in nature given existence by the artist's brush are emerging from the ambient of light and air provided by the surface of the paper itself. Mi Fu's painting could be described as a poetic improvisation on the sombre mood of nature, the haunting vastness of the great panorama only half-revealed through the ghostly veil of clouds: it is a pictorial parallel to Wordsworth's lines on the Simplon Pass:

> Black drizzling crags that spake by the wayside
> As if a voice were in them, the sick sight
> And giddy prospect of the raging stream,
> The unfettered clouds and region of the heavens,
> Tumult and peace, the darkness and the light—
> Were all like workings of one mind, the features
> Of the same face, blossoms upon one tree,

Characters of the great Apocalypse,
The types and symbols of Eternity,
Of first, and last, and midst, and without end.

For comparison with Mi Fu's painting we may select one of Claude
Lorrain's many sketches of the Roman Campagna. These drawings
done in ink and bistre wash were not ends in themselves but were
studies from nature intended to serve as aids in painting a finished composition in the studio. At first glance, the way in which the heavy blobs
of dark wash sparkle on the contrasting white of the paper and the
conception of the main elements of the scene in terms of solid shapes
remind us strongly of Mi Fu and even suggest a Chinese delicacy of
accent. The point of view is one that could be called impressionist
since the artist is interested in catching the effect of light and atmosphere on the surface of things. The very sharpness of the contrasts suggests the blinding radiance of the noonday sun; the solidity and slight
blurring of the dark clumps of foliage not only implies their modeling
in terms of impenetrable shadow but suggests the absorption of trees,
bank, and river in the steaming atmosphere of the Tiber landscape.
What we have in Claude's drawing is an enormously successful setting
down of a direct visual impression in the most effective and laconic
pictorial terms. It is an artist's record of an actual place at an actual
time; what poetry there is in it is inherent in the subject and the artist's
sparkling translation of the theme into the abstract terms of line and
wash. Mi Fu's landscape which, as it now becomes apparent, resem-
bles the Claude drawing only superficially, is in no sense a transcription
of any actual scene. It is something created on the basis of "emotion
recollected in tranquility" [1] and, as the quotation is intended to suggest,
seeks, like a poem, to induce a mood. Although, as in Claude, the means
used to suggest the melancholy grandeur of the scene are the light and
air that enfold the face of nature, what we have is the essence, a symbol,
not a description, of landscape in all its vastness.

6. Men and the Moon

One of the common themes of romantic art is that of man commun-
ing with nature as a revelation of the divine, as a veil cloaking the infinite. The expression of this concept is familiar to us at once in English
lyric poetry and in the writings of Goethe. It is present in Cooper's
description of the American wilderness. This theme finds its expression,
too, in the work of romantic painters both in America and Europe. A
typical example is by the German romantic artist, Caspar David Fried-

[1] William Wordsworth, *Preface to the Lyrical Ballads.*

37. *Two Men in Contemplation of the Moon*

38. *Sage Contemplating the Moon*

rich (1774–1840): "Two Men in Contemplation of the Moon" (figure 37). It is a concept old in Chinese painting as well, and one could find literally scores of variations on the theme. One of the greatest is the picture by Ma Yüan (1190–1224): "Sage Contemplating the Moon" (figure 38).

The comparison of these two paintings that are so similar in their subject matter and mood requires an examination of their background to explain their parallelism. Landscape is the key to German romanticism, where it is used by artists like Friedrich as a mystical and universal symbol of nature, to the extent that the term, spiritualized landscape, was deemed more appropriate than just the designation, landscape, to describe their transcendental content and mood. Landscape became a device for expressing a yearning for the infinite and unknowable through the depth of mood and feeling expressed in the elements of nature comprising the picture. It is not surprising that these symbols—they amount to clichés—include Gothic ruins, rainbows, and auroras, the vasty deep, gnarled oaks, and endless autumn plains stretching to infinity.

Caspar David Friedrich's painting, "Two Men in Contemplation of the Moon," is a perfect embodiment of this point of view. It represents two men standing on a rocky forest eminence, gazing in hypnotic contemplation at the moon rising behind a lacework of branches and roots. The picture is filled with stillness as with the pale effulgence of moonlight. The two figures looking into the picture are a common device of the romantic artists, inviting us to identify ourselves with them and share their reactions to the scene. The magic of the forest setting is conveyed by the familiar twisting of trees and branches, almost as a kind of natural metaphor of Gothic tracery. We sense the old enchantment for the Germanic mind of the mysterious depths of the forest, the world of fairy tales, and the dark Teuton past. The night and the moon, with their obvious symbolic implications of darkness and mystery, are all parts of the paraphernalia that the romantic Gothic artist employs to convey his dominant concern with the infinite strangeness of nature and the suggestion that men fortunate enough to be attuned to the mystery may discern within it the workings of an inner and, at the same time, universal force. Although this picture is perhaps rather obvious, even sentimental, it is in its intent, if not in its realization, a close parallel to the simpler and far more effective expression of the same idea by artists in China.

The painting by Ma Yüan, "Sage Contemplating the Moon" is the exact Oriental counterpart of the romantic point of view. The architecture of the painting is extremely simple. From the left a twisted pine tree stretches its branches over an abyss; behind it at the left is the dim outline of a distant peak. The foreground is the edge of a precipice; on it, a sage reclines in rapt contemplation of the moon and the vast emptiness of space. This painting is a perfect illustration of the so-called one-corner composition. This term comes from the famous parable of Confucius, when the master said: "If I give a man one corner and he cannot come back with the other three, I do not continue the lesson." This parable, which originally had to do with the rectangular layout of rice fields, has been assimilated into Chinese aesthetic terminology. It signifies that, seemingly, the elements actually painted in a picture are concentrated on one side or corner and the rest of the panel is left blank; the beholder is invited to fill in this void and recognize the balance that it forms for the portions of the painting actually defined, in the same way that the object of Confucius' saying was expected instantaneously to bound the complete field. A study of this painting will reveal that, although, indeed, the greater portion of the silk at the right and the upper part of the composition is entirely blank, there are certain compensations for this emptiness. The very eccentricity of the great silhouette of the pine bough stretched across the void of empty distance forms an attraction for the eye that, compositionally, compensates for this blank, and by its prominence suggests the existence of an infinity of space in the background. There are other even more subtle devices employed in this system of occult balance. A kind of psychological unity is established between the upper and lower portions of the painting by the way in which the artist has indicated that the lonely figure is lost in fixed contemplation of the moon that appears diagonally removed from him as a pale disc in the upper right hand corner of the panel. The only indication of movement in a painting dedicated to the vast, enfolding serenity of undisturbed nature is a single cluster of pine needles that falls from the bough and, in its falling, provides another link between the upper and lower halves of the composition. This painting by Ma Yüan is a complete epitome of the romantic point of view toward nature in China. The idea was cultivated by Chinese poets and painters that nature was a revelation of a kind of invisible essence of divine being; nature offered an absorption and peace equivalent to Nirvāna itself and its contemplation could make for forgetfulness in the troubled and transitory world. Nature could present at once a revelation of the divine and the vast serenity of emptiness in the contemplation of which, poet or painter could lose his identity, just as the beholder, in viewing Ma Yüan's picture, could be expected to lose himself in the apprehension of an eternal mystery simply portrayed. The actual vocabulary of pictorial statement in the Ma Yüan painting is as restricted and legible as the compositional formula, and contributes to the succinctness and unity of the formula. A relatively small number of brushstrokes of different shapes and densities of ink are used to set forth laconically and effectively the articulation and texture of elements like the pine tree, the rocks, and the zigzag pattern of the sage's gown. These crisp touches of the brush are set off by the soft, transparent washes that the painter used to suggest the misty infinity of the background. This is a marvellously unified and legible language of pictorial expression, dedicated to the essential poetic aim of presenting man contemplating nature as a veil that masks infinity. The same theme dominates the painting by the German romantic artist, but in his painting we are conscious of a straining for expressiveness, overstatement rather than economy, without the least realization of the effectiveness of what is left unsaid. The parallel we have examined affords us the conclusion that although romantic poetry and romantic painting in the West were philosophically concerned with the same eternal problems of man's relationship to nature, European painters, like Friedrich, with their realistic preoccupations with problems of space, light, and texture failed to convey the sense of divinity in nature which the Chinese artist captured by the minimum of pictorial statement.

7. Art for Art's Sake

In the middle years of the nineteenth century, there occurred a discovery of momentous significance that was to influence profoundly the whole later course of Western painting.

This was the discovery of Japanese art.

It will be remembered that as early as 1853 Commodore Perry with his black ships had forced the opening of Japan to foreign trade. In 1856 a single volume of Hokusai's woodblock prints had found its way to Paris, and it was not long afterward that various connoisseurs discovered that the packages of tea imported from the Secret Empire were wrapped in the most beautiful colored prints which the Japanese at the time considered hardly more valuable than newspapers. By 1862 a shop was opened for the sale of these and other curiosities in Paris. The refinement and aristocratic aloofness, the pure aesthetic satisfaction in design regardless of content found in the Japanese prints, seemed to be what the advocates of art for art's sake had been searching for.

39. *Old Battersea Bridge*

40. *Fireworks at Ryōgoku Bridge*

The concept of *art for art's sake*, which had its inception with the generation of romantic painters and writers of France in the 'thirties of the nineteenth century, means the cultivation of the point of view that art is an end in itself, that, in painting, the artist is justified in the creation of beauty of form or color regardless of meaning or expression—in other words, an art independent of ideas and composed in terms of aesthetic attraction by the abstract arrangement of the elements comprising the picture.

The chief exponent of art for art's sake, both in his life and his art, was James Abbott McNeill Whistler (1834–1903), the expatriate American artist who is remembered for his "Portrait of the Artist's Mother" and for his wit and eccentricity. Whistler, who was trained in the Paris described by du Maurier in *Trilby*, was one of the first Western artists to be influenced by the Japanese print. The idea of a picture, in which the appeal lay in spacing and simple colors and the creation of a mood of delicate poetry in terms of moving line and arresting contour, exercised an inevitable effect on an artist who was already experimenting with compositions in terms of decorative shapes with an emphasis on figures as silhouettes.

The influence of the Japanese print on Whistler's art can best be studied in one of his compositions that is directly based on a Far Eastern prototype. An admirable comparison is that of Whistler's "Battersea Bridge" (figure 39) and Hiroshige's series of prints of "Fireworks at Ryōgoku Bridge" (figure 40).

Although Hiroshige belonged to a generation of Japanese artists that was aware of the technique of Western painting, such as normal perspective and unified lighting, his art is in every way typical of the Far Eastern point of view. The print is composed in terms of line and flat tone. Its beauty rests in the abstract pattern of tonal arrangement in soft neutralized colors. The emotionally arresting incandescent line of the rocket's arc, its asymmetrical balance with the aureole of bursting stars, and the abstract vocabulary of shapes that symbolize the elements in the picture, are all typical of the Oriental expression that we have encountered before. Although prints like this one by Hiroshige at first appear to be cast in a realistic framework, the arrangement of the composition is to all intents and purposes an arbitrary one. The sections devoted to foreground and background in actuality are thought of as flat areas without the implication of any recession in an atmospheric or spatial sense.

What a Japanese print like this one by Hiroshige had chiefly to teach Whistler was a lesson in subdued color and arrangement in flat shapes. Their precedent confirmed him in the idea that any illusion of the third dimension was simply a vulgar mistake of Western painting and that the true artist should concern himself with decorative arrangements in flat tone and the evocation of a mood of beauty through the organization of shapes and tonal patterns on the surface of the canvas.

Paintings like the "Battersea Bridge" belong to a class that Whistler described as Nocturnes. It seems likely that Whistler chose this designation deliberately because the word, Nocturne, would recall the form of musical composition immortalized by Haydn and Chopin: the suggestion in this title of the abstract quality of music would only stress the artist's interest in tonal and compositional harmony and his lack of concern with subject matter.

The relationship between the "Battersea Bridge" and Hiroshige's "Fireworks at Ryōgoku Bridge" is rather obvious in the placing of the flat, silhouette of the bridge against the night sky and the asymmetrical balance in the shower of rockets in the upper right-hand corner. Like all of Whistler's Nocturnes the picture is painted in an extremely limited range of color with a deliberate suppression of color contrast and the contrast of light and shade. In this respect, and also in the conscious transposition of reality for the sake of both decorative and emotional expressiveness, the Whistler composition shows the influence of Hiroshige.

The actual structure of the bridge has been enormously attenuated; it is no more than a shape of some strange, indefinable dream fabric looming against the rocket-strewn sky. By a deliberate exaggeration of the Hiroshige formula the spatial relationships of the different parts of the picture are ambiguous: foreground and background are co-extensive flat areas existing only as patterns on the surface of the canvas. We feel that in pictures like the "Battersea Bridge" Whistler was interested not only in experimentation in tonal harmony in a minor key but in the romantic suggestion of that moment of evening enchantment when the "mist clothes the riverside with poetry as with a veil, and the poor buildings lose themselves in the dim sky, and the tall chimneys become campanili, and the warehouses are palaces in the night, and the whole city hangs in the heavens and fairyland is before us." [1]

While there is nothing novel or startling about Whistler's point of view today, it stirred up a tremendous controversy in London in the 'sixties, a time when the subject-picture, a mixture of bathos and almost mechanically perfect finish, was accepted as the highest form of art. Whistler had no interest in subjects or mechanical finish. His attitude

[1] Theodore Duret, *Whistler* (London: G. Richards, 1917), p. 45.

was completely similar to that of the French painters and writers in believing that art provided its own justification. A painting needed no story, no literary or historical background, no implications of social reform.

To the painters and critics of late nineteenth-century Paris, Whistler's pictures evoked the quality of pure music, the ephemeral, dreamlike quality that characterizes the poetry of Mallarmé and Verlaine. This was not at all surprising, since both the poetry of Verlaine and the painting of Whistler represented the final step in the severance of art from everyday life and its withdrawal to a sanctuary of pure form intended for the initiate alone. The very qualities of obscurity and incompleteness that so annoyed Whistler's enemy, the critic John Ruskin, brought the greatest praise from the high priest of the decadence, J. K. Huysmans:

These scenes of air and water extend to infinity, they suggest dandlings of the fancy, transport us on magic carpets through time immeasurable to extramundane spheres. They are beyond everything, on the extreme boundaries of painting, which in these slight canvases seem to evaporate in ethereal coloured smoke.[1]

If, as it sometimes seems, Whistler's reputation has itself "evaporated into ethereal colored smoke," it must be remembered that in many respects he is the true forerunner of what we think of as modern painting. His deliberate distortion of spatial relationship, his reduction of visual reality to abstract pattern in terms of both color and shape, forecast the work of John Marin, whose landscape will be analyzed in Chapter Two(8). What is chiefly important to us in the comparison with Hiroshige is that it was precisely the elements present in the Oriental prototype that Whistler exploited in the interests of his own interpretation of reality in terms of heightened emotional and aesthetic attraction through the reduction of actuality to expressively decorative shapes and tones.

8. *Expressionists in Landscape*

The comparisons which are often made between the work of twentieth-century water colorists like John Marin (1870–1953) and the more explosive of the Chinese ink landscape paintings have a certain validity in that both are very personal interpretations, recorded in what some critics like to call an individual shorthand or calligraphy. Beyond this and the common looseness of handling, the comparison is

[1] Duret, *Whistler*, p. 118.

a misleading one, since in the final analysis the aim and technique are as separate as the works are geographically and in time.

If we compare a typical Marin water color like the "Maine Islands" (figure 41) with the ink painting of a "Mountain Village" (figure 42) by the thirteenth-century Chinese painter, Ying Yü-chien, we are struck by the superficial resemblance in the immediate impact of the composition in terms of startling, even staccato accents of dark on the white paper, the moving, almost disorganized presentation of the scene. Let us examine the reasons for this similarity. Marin is an artist who, by his own statement, has been fascinated by the constantly moving pattern of change on the face of nature, as seen in the movement of clouds, trees, waves, shifting lights, surging water, and the dramatic massing and conflict of buildings in a great city. As his critics tell us, he has devised an appropriately rapid technique to express this reaction, a method that is partly impressionistic in its concern for representing light in terms of color, and partly abstract in the character of the strokes used to describe the pictorial elements. Marin is an artist who began as a rather mediocre follower in the Whistler tradition. Briefly, the Whistler manner of painting landscape was to represent the scene with objects lost in haze and light, reduced to a simplified, almost flat design, with a completely arbitrary disarrangement of normal space relationships. On this formula which begins with a recording of a given scene at a given moment as the artist sees it in terms of light and air, Marin has superimposed certain mannerisms of his own in the shape of very swift, seemingly careless definitions of elements like trees, rocks, and mountains in choppy brushstrokes of varying shapes that form a dancing pattern on the surface of the paper. When successful, the effect is that of the dazzling, startling brilliance of light itself with a recording in abstract terms of the kaleidoscopic movement and change that our eyes discern in sea and land in brilliant sunlight. For all the excitement of the result, there is always an inconsistency in this marriage of impressionism and abstraction. And the very rapidity of execution and the unpredictable accidents in the medium often produce digressions that are annoying because of their illegibility.

Things like inconsistency and illegibility are no part of the Chinese tradition of landscape painting. For all their abbreviation of statement there is always complete control.

The landscape, "Mountain Village," is the work of a painter attached to the Ch'an or Zen sect of Buddhism that saw the attainment of the individual's security and serenity in his intuitive realization of his relation to the world, from the greatest mountain to the least flower.

41. *Maine Islands*

42. *Mountain Village*

This perception of one's unity and kinship came in a flash of instantaneous, often irrational, intuition. Such explosions of recognition in the mind demand an instantaneity of technique to set down the vision before it fades. The present Chinese landscape is a breathless, electrifying recording of such a fleeting glimpse of what is permanent behind the façade of nature. It is the result of a discipline of hand to eye and mind, not willful disorder, but a completely consistent order in the arrangement and texture of the sparse elements of setting that present a fleeting revelation of the universal order in this little piece of nature. Although there is some resemblance to Marin's technique in the shorthand quality and the way in which the forms seem to float upon the surface of the paper, the resemblance ends there, because every section of the Chinese landscape is legible and part of a wonderfully contrived unity in the broken patterns and snapping variations of ink, tone, and value. This unity is achieved through the artist's handling of the medium of ink wash and his exploitation of the behavior of the various blotches and splashes of ink that comprise the picture. Each one of these seemingly carelessly adumbrated areas stands for some element in nature and is tied to the whiplike deployment of the path leading into the distance of the picture. The soft mergence and emergence of the forms from the paper suggest the sensation of the change and movement in the face of nature in the light and air that alternately veil and clarify the appearance of reality. This painting represents an enormously economical concentration without the slightest irrelevancy and has nothing whatever to do with any kind of self-conscious expressionistic presentation. Over and beyond the marvelous pattern that the picture presents in terms of the rich black tone on the surface of the paper, the wonderful thing about this painting is the connotation of the feeling of the constant process of change, the whole shifting pattern of nature set down in shapes that appear to dissolve in the pools of ink and at the same time take on the form of recognizable elements that fit into a perfectly logical pattern in space and texture. This unity and this marvelously succinct suggestion of dynamic movement in landscape make the Marin formula seem thin and merely decorative in comparison.

Chapter Three

Birds, Beasts, and Flowers

THE term, bird-and-flower painting, is used to describe a type of painting that could be regarded as a subsidiary of genre or still life. Both in the Orient and the West the subject has been treated in a symbolic and realistic fashion.

The bird as a frail and perfect aerial vessel has, from the beauty of its flight and articulation, come to represent a symbol of freedom and spiritual release. The very beauty of the flower, too, in the loveliness of its growth and its appeal to both the senses and the spirit, has been an emblem for poets and artists of something beyond the material world. In the contemplation of such little things, some artists have expressed their feelings about the all-inclusive parenthood of nature. At the same time, the very textural attractions of birds and flowers have recommended themselves to artists interested in a purely objective recording of the beauty of their outward appearance in terms of paint, in other words, a form of magic realism.

Until comparatively recent times Europeans have not felt at home in nature in the way that Chinese poets and painters have always expressed their affinity for the oneness of all natural objects. Nature in the West has been either an object of fear or exploitation. Although occasionally used as a symbol, like the goldfinch, the bird for most Europeans is something to put in a cage or in a cooking pot, or, since the Renaissance, one more object of scientific curiosity, a revelation of one of those myriad facets of the living world that modern man has begun to explore. For Dürer a dead bluebird provides an admirable subject for the microscopic textural definition of plumage. Neither for this artist nor for most Renaissance painters is there the slightest interest in the bird as a thing of beauty for itself, as a fragile emblem of flight, or harbinger of spring. It is only with the poetry of the romantic period in the West that we encounter a spiritual approximation to the Far Eastern regard for nature both from the point of view of landscape and the beauty of birds and beasts.

> Little flower—but if I could understand
> What you are, root and all, and all in all,
> I should know what God and man is.

These lines of Tennyson express the same mystery and awe of the workings of the universe revealed in its smallest manifestation that we know in Taoism and Zen Buddhism. Something of that same awareness of nature is expressed in William Blake's poem,

> How do you know but ev'ry Bird that cuts the airy way,
> Is an immense World of Delight, clos'd by your senses five?

It is this recognition of the slightest thing in nature as an emblem and exemplar of the spirit and growth of all life that most closely unites the thought of the romantic poets in Europe and the poets and painters of China.

For the Chinese artist, in painting birds, it is necessary to suggest not only the architecture of their plumage but the airy lightness of their movement; he will strive to catch the relentless pounce of the hawk, the weightless fluttering of sparrows and magpies in endless, busy commotion. The Chinese painter is more interested in suggesting the universal idea of the action and articulation of birds as a small revelation of the ever-renewed creative process of nature than in the scientific distinctions of various categories of the species. In Chinese art birds are symbols of seasons and moods: the magpie, the herald of good luck and gladness; the dove as an emblem of the amorous awakening of spring.

From very early times Chinese connoisseurs arranged paintings in grades of excellence according to subject matter with the highest rank invariably reserved for the painting of human figures. Birds and flowers together do not form a special group in this hierarchy but are listed separately. In the tenth century, paintings of birds and animals were rated second only to human figures and above the category reserved for landscapes. Paintings of flowers and plants are generally placed below the representations of "feathers and fur" in the estimate of Chinese critics of art.

There have been painters of birds, beasts, and flowers in every period of Chinese art who have used this subject matter for a great variety of artistic expression: for its philosophic and symbolic implications; as a technical exercise from the realistic point of view; and as a point of departure for the display of technical virtuosity in ink and wash. In all of these modes of expression the principal criterion has been based not so much on outward verisimilitude in the scientific manner of a Dürer or a Pisanello, but rather on the suggestion of the dynamic inner life and articulation peculiar to the thing represented.

Something should be said at this point regarding the Chinese painter's understanding and use of what we define as realism. Although we are accustomed to thinking of the Chinese artist's drawing from memory in the manner of both medieval and Renaissance painters in the West, drawing from life was by no means unknown in the Orient. There is a Chinese term *hsieh shêng* which means literally, drawing from life, and is used to describe the artist's depiction of animals, birds, or flowers. Another term, *ch'üan shên* (take a likeness), is usually reserved for portraiture, but as early as the Sung period (960–1279 A.D.) its meaning extended to the representation of all things in nature. Both of these definitions imply more than a careful copying of the details of natural objects. The word *shên* in the second compound means indwelling spirit; so that, actually, these definitions of realism are not separate from the concept expressed by the First Principle of Chinese painting, formulated by Hsieh Ho in the fifth century, and already discussed in Chapter One(4). For even this seemingly academic stressing of texture and detail has for its final aim the presentation of the essential aliveness appropriate to its species. Although it is recorded that all the classic masters of the Five Dynasties and early Sung periods drew from life, the early critics invariably praised them for infusing an appropriate life movement into their painted creations.

The term *ch'i-yün shêng-tung*, which has been the subject of so much rhapsodizing and misinterpretation by amateurs of Oriental art, contains the essence of the Chinese aesthetic of painting. It means far more than the meaningless term, rhythmic vitality, sometimes given as a translation. It means that an artist, by observation and intuition, shall properly represent a given living thing with the kind of life movement, *shêng tung*—the action, gait, or pose peculiar to his painted creature—that will give the impression of its being appropriately imbued (*yün*, harmony) with its own vibrant life, or breath, or spirit (*ch'i*). The great seventeenth-century artist, Tao Chi, remarked: "In painting trees one must make them grow." This is obviously a procedure that involves a kind of self-identification on the part of the artist with his subject, so that, being it, he can create it. As Dante said, "He who would paint a figure, if he cannot be it cannot draw it." It is this quality that is implicit in the Chinese stories of painted dragons so enlivened that they soared away, or the paintings of pheasants so real that they deceived the imperial falcons into pouncing on these likenesses.

In the painting of living things, as in every other category of the art, the other principles of Chinese painting, such as the definition of structure through brushstroke, appropriate verisimilitude, approximation of natural color, and compositional arrangement, are all of them only the means necessary to the end of realizing the first and most important aim of infusing a feeling of appropriate and stirring animation into the subject.

1. *Audubon and a Sung Master*

Comparisons of Chinese bird paintings with their Western counterparts are particularly illuminating for an explanation of both the technique and the intent of the artist, if only because the very limitation of the subject matter makes the analysis easier and clearer. If we compare the "Parakeet on a Blossoming Pear Branch" (figure 44) by a follower of the Emperor Hui Tsung (1082–1135) [1] with the study of the "Carolina Parakeet" (figure 43) by the great American painter, Jean-Jacques Audubon (1785–1851), we shall find certain telling differences and resemblances in presentation that are the inevitable result of the place and time of their production.

Our first impression of the Chinese painting is that of a very concentrated representation of the bird in terms of precise drawing and a painstaking regard for the elements of color, texture, and form.

[1] The picture is an anonymous production of an artist of the Southern Sung period (1127–1280).

We notice, too, how the bird on its flowering pear branch is carefully placed in relationship to the empty silk that envelops the subject.

The technique could be described as a refined magic realism in which the bird is drawn with the brush in fine contour lines and literally every feather is precisely defined in its appropriate shape and color. There is no modeling and no real suggestion of texture, but the plumage has a kind of iridescence from the subtle gradations in value in each area. Taken as a whole, the parakeet is merely a colored silhouette. Both the bird, the branch that supports it, and the aureole of blossoms exist entirely on the picture plane like a screen of shapes against the empty background.

The "Parakeet on a Blossoming Pear Branch," however, possesses more than an exquisite but empty decorative quality; the little creature has an animation and a distinct character of its own, an air of imminent flight and alertness from its curved beak to the beautifully drawn talons gripping the branch. In the relationship of the painted shapes and the empty silk at the right of the panel we have another example of the Chinese artist's use of an asymmetrical balance that we have already investigated under the heading of landscape painting.

The "Carolina Parakeet" appears first and foremost as a painting done with the scientific intent of recording the appearance of an exotic species. This picture was executed in pencil line and water color with a suggestion of modeling both in the bird and the leaves that causes these shapes to stand out in relief on the page. The pictorial elements more or less fill the available space of the paper, and there is no suggestion of the asymmetrical composition of the Sung painting. Although Audubon's work might be more realistic than its Chinese counterpart, in certain respects its treatment is more generalized in the suppression of details and the concentration on the essential factors of form and design. Audubon was an artist who had become so identified with the birds and the vanished American wilderness which they inhabited, that in an intuitive romantic way he was able to confer upon them something of the personality peculiar to the species; so that his animation of the parakeet exploring its little world of leaves and berries approximates the recording of the dignity and poise that the Chinese painter saw in the rare bird from the Indies. One could say that Audubon was perhaps more concerned with the exact distinctions of shape and plumage that distinguish his subject, but the dramatic aliveness of the subject transcends mere literal transcription. The Sung artist in the rather flat and even patternized painting of the bird on his floral perch, was more concerned with communicating in terms of exquisite soft-

43. *Carolina Parakeet*

44. *Parakeet on a Blossoming Pear Branch*

ness of color and calculated spatial arrangement a poetic memento of the beauty of spring as he saw it revealed in the iridescent parakeet perched on the flowering pear bough.

The solitary bird on its branch is conceived in serenity and isolation as a symbol of the unchanging immortality of things in nature's world. This isolation, both pictorial and spiritual, is achieved by the subtle balance between the painted form and the vast emptiness of the silk; and the way in which the whole design exists as a flat silhouette on the picture plane is a means of projecting the subject to the beholder without the distractions of depth or atmosphere.

2. *Little Things in Nature*

In the history of Chinese painting the scroll of "Early Autumn" (figure 46) by Ch'ien Hsüan (1235–1290), an artist of the Yüan period (1279–1368) marks a high point in the realistic definition of things in the world of nature. Whether this realism is to be explained as an outgrowth of the exquisite academic realism already exemplified by the Sung artist, or as a reflection of the intensely practical, and anything but poetic, civilization introduced by the Mongol conquerors of China, is beside the point. The fact remains that even within this marvelous counterfeiting of a little landscape of lotuses and grasses populated by a host of insects, there is still, as in the Sung painting, more poetry than truth. The realism of this scroll consists in the astonishing aliveness of the grasshoppers and dragonflies recorded with a wonderful sense of their fragility and lightness, and extends to a suggestion of actual light and hazy atmosphere in the pale orange glow of the background and the gradual diminution of contrasts in the jungle of weeds and leaves that provides the stage. No Western artist, except perhaps Dürer, would have thought of conferring such pains on these transient inhabitants of the summer grasses. True, we occasionally find insects in Western art: pinks and columbines, juniper, and fluttering butterflies tapestry the background of Pisanello's portrait of Ginevra d'Este,[1] but they are there only as poetic reminders of the springtime freshness of the girl herself. In Ch'ien Hsüan's scroll the insects are there for themselves alone, and we, in a way, are forced to enter into their life because of the point of view from which the artist has painted the scene, as though he himself were a part of their little world. Notice the animated and exact portrait of the katydid. Over and beyond the wonderful recording of this microcosm, the picture is a kind of lyric evoca-

[1] Cf. René Huyghe, *Art Treasures of the Louvre* (New York: H. N. Abrams, 1951), plate 7.

tion of a seasonal mood and the poetic suggestion of the golden hazy light of autumn; the frayed, withering leaves and dying grasses imply that the drowsy insects existing in this final warmth of summer will soon fade and sleep.

Many people will say, why not compare this painting with some of those precise recordings of little bits of nature by the great German Renaissance artist, Albrecht Dürer (1471–1528)? And a natural subject for comparison is Dürer's famous water color, "The Great Piece of Turf" (figure 45). What we have in Dürer's picture is a really wonderful microscopic representation of every leaf and stem in the intricate forest of weeds and grasses. The comparison with the Ch'ien Hsüan scroll indicates clearly that Dürer could not see the clump for the grasses. To be sure, flowers, weeds, and grasses are there, individually recorded with an amazing precision and intricacy of arrangement. But where is that suggestion of actual growth in flying lines of wash that, in the Ch'ien Hsüan, make the grasses bend and the lotus fronds rattle in the wind? Where is the suggestion of atmosphere and filtered light, the complete legibility of the most intricate passages? Where is the evocation of the transcience of all nature that makes Ch'ien Hsüan's picture more than a botanical study? Perhaps the answer is that Dürer did not know what it was like to be a tuft of grass blowing and bobbing in the wind, nor to feel himself a grasshopper balanced on a quivering blade. Dürer was interested in recording what the physical eye saw, and not, like the Oriental artist, in revealing more than the eye discerned.

Dürer's painting, for all its accomplishment, belongs to a period in the development of Western art when the artist was unable to depart from the strictly empirical accuracy of his representation of natural forms to suggest their organic growth. It is precisely this inability to reconcile scientific observation and vitalization of the subject that gives the great German artist's pictures of living things an air of still-life painting. In later chapters on Botticelli and Leonardo da Vinci we shall encounter painters whose dynamic animation of animal and plant forms is spiritually more akin to the Far Eastern point of view.

3. Falcons

The comparison between the drawing of a falcon by Pisanello (ca. 1380–1455) (figure 47) and the miniature of the same subject by the seventeenth-century Mogul painter, Mansur (figure 48), is one in which it appears more difficult to find differences than likenesses. Both are very precise representations of an ornithological subject with

45. *The Great Piece of Turf*

46. *Early Autumn* (*detail*)

48. *Falcon*

47. *Hooded Falcon*

a microscopic regard for the outward details of the model. Although these two paintings appear so very similar, it is precisely the analysis of their divergence in artistic presentation that makes the comparison worthwhile.

The peregrine drawn by Pisanello is one of a number of such studies done in the mews from a natural bird. The technique is a combination of ink and water color, in which the silhouette of the bird, and each individual feather, is outlined with the pen and then filled in with a brown pigment to suggest the appropriate local tone and texture. Both the body of the bird and its blue hood are given a slight suggestion of modeling. The whole strikes one as an entirely objective recording of a hawk, completely successful in its evocation of both texture and form within a limited medium. There is no artistic interpretation, properly speaking, beyond what is inherent in the subject in the anonymity and mystery conferred by the hood.

The falcon by the Emperor Jehāngīr's court painter, Mansur, could certainly be described as a realistic representation, too. The realism practiced by Mogul court artists, although, perhaps, influenced by what the painters had seen of European pictures brought to India by the Jesuits, is also the result of that boredom with ideality expressed by one of Jehāngīr's nobles: "Let the poets and artists take for their subjects what we have ourselves seen and heard." There is every reason to believe that the bird here portrayed was a rare falcon that particularly delighted Mansur's patron, the Emperor Jehāngīr.[1]

What strikes us first of all in this miniature is the exquisite clarity and precision in the definition of every detail. The artist's approach is perhaps to be described as conceptual, since the total image of the bird is a collection of individually painted feathers, without any real concern for the organic structure of the whole. Another factor that militates against a completely realistic representation is that whatever subject the Mogul painter draws is always presented within the bounding contour that defines it, so that every detail of the structure is essentially pinned to the picture plane, regardless of its relative position forward or back. This consciousness of pattern, expressed in outline, is not in any sense an Indian or a Western device, but is probably to be explained as an inheritance from the tradition of Persian miniature painting. Persian artists of all periods reduced the forms of nature to mag-

[1] "What can I write of the beauty and color of this falcon? As it was something out of the common, I ordered Ustad Mansur, who has the title of Wonder of the Age, to paint and preserve its likeness." Alexander Rogers (trans.), *Memoirs of Jehāngīr*, ed. Henry Beveridge (London: Royal Asiatic Society, 1909–1914), II, 107.

nificent linear, heraldic conventions in the formation of a style that made the world of pictures an entirely magic one, separate in its artificial serenity and fantasy from the world of reality.

The one salient contrast between these two similar treatments of a single object from nature is the more generalized and, at the same time, more scientific accuracy of Pisanello. This is to be explained by the scientific tenor of his age, in its universal concentrated searching for truth in the very least element of the nature that surrounds us. Although the equal of Mansur in the meticulous definition of texture and pattern, Pisanello was primarily concerned with producing an accurate presentation of the idea of the falcon, rather than the portrait of a particular bird. The ability to see and present real things in an objective manner is a specifically Western development of the Renaissance and later. The realism of the Mogul artist, regardless of the subject matter he painted, was always intuitive and particular, rather than scientific and general; and it is precisely this, together with his magnificent feeling for abstract pattern, that separates the performance of the Indian from the European painter.

For Mogul artists, recording the comforting reality of little incidents and things that interrupted the routine of life at the court was more important than the repetition of standard themes of Indian epic legend. Pisanello's study of a falcon was one of many realistic details intended to make a credible contemporary happening out of the painter's imagining of an episode from sacred legend.

4. *Proud Steeds*

A type of comparison somewhat different from the parallels already discussed is an analysis of the accepted standards of performance in Eastern and Western art in a restricted category. Such a comparison should bring out distinctly the essential likenesses and differences in the technique and ideals of East and West. For the purposes of such a comparison we may examine the representations of the horse by two of the most famous artists in the traditions of the West and East: Leonardo da Vinci (1452–1519), the inimitable painter and scientist of the Renaissance, and Han Kan, the great *animalier* of the T'ang Dynasty (618–906 A.D.) in China. Both artists (figures 49 and 50), in their different ways, respond to the nobility of the theme—a creature which, in the traditions of both East and West, was regarded as second only to man in intelligence and bearing.

Leonardo is remembered as an artist of universal inclination, one for whom the certainty of science replaced earlier reliance on divine

inspiration. For Leonardo, science, not God determined genius. It is
not surprising that we find an affirmation of this in the least sketch that
left his hands. It is most manifest in his sketches of animals and growing things that presented a challenge both for the record of scientific
observation and the employment of that observation and knowledge,
to suggest the peculiarities of action and life that Leonardo discerned
in the actual model. All Leonardo's drawings of horses reveal a searching for a norm of perfection second only to his lifelong experiment in
the architecture and articulation of human bodies. Leonardo is credited
with having evolved a canon of proportion for the anatomy of horses.
This unfortunately has been lost, but his drawings survive to indicate
his intended ideal. In this one department of Leonardo's universal creation, scientific observation is, as always, the scaffold of imaginative
ideation. Of all the drawings of horses, both for paintings and equestrian
monuments, that filled Leonardo's notebooks, the most aesthetically
moving are always those of ethereal wild horses with twisted necks and
foaming manes that move in the spectral transparency of Leonardo's
silverpoint technique. They, far more than the admirable studies from
life, reveal Leonardo's genius to impart what he called artificial liveli-
ness where none existed in the model. This is, in other words, an illustration of that dynamic animation and suggestion of inner life that mo-
tivates Leonardo's studies of human figures. Even more significant of
his style is the fondness for contortion and for twisting the anatomy in
curve and countercurve—a disturbing linear rhythm, not only for decorative purposes, but precisely for the revelation of that peculiar life
and spirit that Leonardo saw in the animal mechanism. These distortions
are all directed to evoke the pride and impetuosity, the pliant and steel
strength that Leonardo recognized as the dominant characteristics of
the horse. Here, as always in Leonardo's performance, the realization is
very strictly based on a completely scientific knowledge of anatomical
function, and the result is only an imaginative heightening of actual
structural form.

The reader may well ask, what has this analysis of the essentially
scientific bias of Leonardo and his drawing to do with the standard of
representing horses in Chinese art, as exemplified by Han Kan? One
has only to compare Leonardo's drawing with the painting by Han
Kan to see how both artists in admittedly different techniques succeeded in evoking a suggestion of impetuosity and virility, so that both
are in a way ideographs of the horse in a universal sense. The analysis
of the likenesses and differences between the two belong to our analysis
of the Chinese painting.

49. *Study for the Adoration of the Kings*

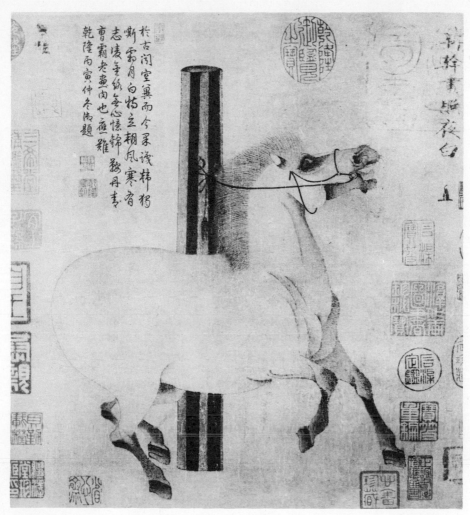

50. *Horse*

Han Kan, who lived in the eighth century, has always been regarded as the great classic Chinese painter of horses. He served the
Emperor Ming Huang in the capacity of portraitist of the royal stables.
At this moment in Chinese history the imperial stud contained thou-
sands of horses from every region of Asia, collected not only for their
utility in military use and recreation, but as objects of virtu no less
prized than the imperial concubines for their grace and strength and
agility. In the Chinese literature of that time the sagacity and power of
horses is frequently a metaphor for the deportment of courtiers and
statesmen. Since the work of Han Kan's masters is entirely unknown to
us, the literary accounts of his artistic training are completely meaningless. There is, however, a famous legend of his artistic beginnings
that sheds a peculiar light on his art. It is related that when the Emperor questioned Han Kan on his training, the artist replied, "All the
horses in Your Majesty's stables are my teachers." The name of Han
Kan has become a kind of generic term for the attribution of Chinese
horse paintings in all periods, although only a handful of pictures surviving today can be associated with his style. One of these is a small
scroll representing "Star of the Night," one of the famous steeds in the
imperial collection. This painting with a pedigree going back to the
ninth century is generally regarded as a possible original from the artist's hand. It is evident, however, that only the head and foreparts of
the horse in the drawing have escaped damage and weak retouching.

The archaic appearance of Han Kan's horse may at first seem surprising in view of the great sophistication of T'ang art in the realm of
figure painting both religious and secular. It will become apparent that
what we think of as archaic in the presentation is, rather, a cultivated
simplicity, dedicated to quite other ends than naturalism or even organic articulation. We are all aware that primitive artists in drawing
animals usually present them as symbols of their one dominant quality
in which they are superior to man and the object of his admiration. By
various distortions of shape and movement the antelope becomes an
ideograph of flight, the elephant of massive strength, or the tiger of
snarling ferocity. Han Kan's painting of a horse is, in a sense, a deliberate and sophisticated perpetuation of this point of view, because he
has limited himself to stressing the fierce pride of the steed as a symbol
of impetuosity of strength that cannot be broken. He has done this by
expressing in terms of tensile outline the arched power of the neck, the
streaming mane and distended nostrils, and the restless pawing of the
hooves, without any special regard for the integration of these features
as parts of a mechanism, such as Leonardo would have given us. What

strike us first in looking at the drawing are the flaming mane, the square, craggy eye, and the distended nostrils that ideographically convey the spirit of the subject. The figure of the horse is drawn in lines so sharp that they appear almost like incisions in the plane of the paper. These outlines are slightly reinforced by a soft and graduated shading, and the effect is that of a shallow relief in a number of overlapping planes, rather than a shape conceived of in the round. Isolated as it is against the entirely blank background, Han Kan's horse is another illustration of how Chinese painters deliberately restricted their subjects to a single plane, as though by this device they intended to project the subject to the beholder in terms of an affecting and animated silhouette. We have seen how Leonardo conferred a sense of nobility and dynamic action upon his animals through the implication of life and movement in his perfect integration of their anatomical mechanism. Han Kan, the master of this same subject in Chinese art, was interested in animation rather than in anatomy, in spirit rather than in substance, and achieved his result without science by stressing those features of the subject that are essential to it and universal in its conception.

5. *Picasso Anticipated*

One of the most famous painters of the Yüan Dynasty, renowned particularly as an animalier, was the fourteenth-century master, Chao Mêng-fu (1254–1322). What is certainly one of his greatest paintings is a short hand-scroll in the collection of the Freer Gallery of Art, Washington, D.C. (figure 52). The subject is a sheep and a goat, drawn in monochrome ink with a short explanatory note by the artist that may be translated as follows: "I often paint horses, but very seldom sheep. When Chung Shin asked me to paint, I amused myself by making a picture from life; and though I could not equal the men of old, it contains real spirit harmony." What the artist meant by saying that his creations were filled with spirit harmony (ch'i-yün) is that he has been able to imbue these commonplace animals with the pose and movement and form that we can recognize instinctively as completely appropriate to their species: from the point of view of structure, texture, and characteristic attitude, the sheep is completely sheeplike and the goat satisfyingly goatlike. The ability to suggest an appropriate life movement or aliveness through appropriate articulation, rather than to attempt to copy outward appearance, has always been the first principle of Chinese painting. In Chao Mêng-fu's painting the animals are drawn as though capable of imminent movement. They are drawn with the greatest economy of brushstroke, a technique which, in its combination of

51. *Ram*

52. *Ram and Goat*

ink wash and dry brush, suggests both texture and structure. This is a performance that is the result not only of a consummate mastery of the medium, but also of the ability of the artist to have the essentials of forms observed in nature so fixed in his mind that he can create them in painting and endow them with life.

An admirable comparison for this Oriental masterpiece is the aquatint of a ram (figure 51) drawn by the twentieth-century painter, Pablo Picasso, for an edition of Buffon's *Histoire naturelle*. This is a presentation that an Oriental artist would understand, the perfect realization of the essential nature of the animal: the texture of its heavy fleece, the solid, virile strength of its body. Everything that is necessary to say about a ram is there. A combination of flowing line and ink fingerprints are the Western equivalent of Chao Mêng-fu's brushwork in the perfect and economical suggestion of both texture and structure. Like the Chinese painting this is a kind of drawing that results from a complete knowledge of technique and the artist's capacity to define the essential features peculiar to a given subject—the specific qualities of articulation that endow it with the breath of life.

6. *The Image in the Rock*

"To that instrument of the subconscious, the hand of a sculptor, there exists an image within every rock. The creative act of realization merely frees it."[1] These words, written by the late John Flannagan (1895–1942), might be applied to describe the technique and the aesthetic effect of Indian sculpture in many different periods, most notably, the gigantic eighth-century carving of the "Descent of the Ganges" at Māmallapuram, and the freestanding groups of sculpture associated with it. Indeed, the resemblance between certain details, such as the "Monkey Family" at Māmallapuram (figure 54) and a similar subject by the American sculptor (figure 53), is so close that one might almost think these two pieces are works of the same school.

For Flannagan, a true stone-carver, the problem was always to preserve the identity of the original rock, and at the same time, by devices of simplification that respect the material, to suggest the very distilled essence of the form and spirit of the creatures freed from the rock by his chisel. This suggestion of the form's literal emergence from the imprisoning matter was for him a way of suggesting in plastic language the stirrings of the life process, "realizing in visible form, the pro-

[1] *The Sculpture of John Flannagan*, ed. Dorothy C. Miller (New York: Museum of Modern Art, 1942), pp. 7 f.

found subterranean urge of the human spirit in the whole dynamic life process—birth, growth, decay, death."

The fascination for him of the idea of birth, becoming, and change, to be suggested by forms struggling to be born where the sculptor's eye espied them, was, in the work of Flannagan, a Western parallel to the realization of the idea of *māya* in the sculpture of India. Māya in Indian philosophy is the universal, undifferentiated substance, from which all beings—divine, human, and animal—have their birth, continually merging in, and emerging from, the cosmic essence.

In Indian art of all periods sculptors have, in varying degrees, been concerned with the suggestion of the apparition of living form out of the formless primal substance by the device of leaving the carving unfinished, or in relief presenting the forms as bosses literally emerging or swelling out of the stone. In the great relief representing the "Descent of the Ganges," we have a late and magnificent example of this technique, so that the granite seems literally to transform itself into individualized and animate forms. In the "Monkey Family," which is a freestanding group set in front of the great cliff that upholds the main relief, we have, as in the same subject by Flannagan, the powerful suggestion that these only partially adumbrated shapes are not completely released from the imprisoning stone. In both cases the carver's retention of the "identity of the original rock" through the very roughness of the surfaces and the appropriately rocklike representation of the forms is the technical factor that imparts this impression of the forms gradually emerging and materializing before our eyes. This is a treatment that at the same time, through simplification, bestows an enormous weightiness and dignity on the creatures portrayed—in the present subject matter, imbuing the monkeys with absorption in themselves, what Flannagan described as the "ironic pensiveness of the apparently thoughtful monkey." It is at once the feeling of emergence, and a suggestion of that peculiar individual life force and form that differentiates one living species from another, which in a parallel way is the aim and effect realized by both sculptors—as Flannagan said, "through the austere elimination of the accidental for ordered simplification [to] embrace all living forms, each for its plastic adjustment to a theme."

There is no question of influence here. Flannagan never went to India and, so far as we know, was unacquainted with Indian sculpture. The comparison illustrates how artists, completely removed from one another in space and time, independently develop similar technical expedients for the realization of essentially similar philosophic and aesthetic ideals.

53. *Monkey Family*

54. *Monkey Family*

7. *The Inner Eye*

A book of comparisons like the present one should rightly include a sampling of the work of Western artists who profess to have been influenced by Oriental material, in order to demonstrate the likenesses and differences of this kinship. A case in point is the painting of the contemporary artist, Morris Graves (1910–   ), who has always admitted to a profound influence from the art of the Orient. This artist's paintings are executed almost entirely in monochrome water color and gouache on the thinnest of rice paper, a technique calculated to suggest both the tonality and fragility of Oriental paintings on silk. Another common denominator which is frequently pointed out is the calligraphic character of this artist's brushwork. The term, *calligraphic*, as used by Western art critics signifies a recognized pattern or structure in the individual lines comprising a picture and something like the flourish or movement of brushstrokes that is supposed to be comparable to Oriental painting. Although all of these borrowings are useful to this painter in developing a personal style, they are, in actuality, only superficially related to the Chinese and Japanese tradition of painting.

Morris Graves describes his paintings as Visions of the Inner Eye, by which one is to understand that they are glimpses of the subconscious automatically transferred to paper. They are, perhaps, to be understood as expressions of the artist's feeling of man's kinship with the fleeting creatures of the wild. Whereas Audubon's paintings of birds are illustrative of man's romantic search for the strange and exotic at the farthest frontiers of the material world, Graves's birds are creatures seen on journeys down the labyrinthine depths of the artist's mind at the frontiers of the subconscious. Such an approach is, perhaps, completely typical of an artist in the atomic age, when the romantic's only escape from sickening external reality is in the secret heart of his own psyche. Graves seems to be expressing in a personal symbolic language his feeling for the ecstatic joys and sufferings of birds and beasts and their inevitable absorption or disintegration in the everchanging substance of nature. One could say this was for Graves a Western equivalent of māya, expressed in dark washes or phosphorescent webs, in which the creatures of his mind are enfolded.

In a painting by Graves like the "Wounded Gull" (figure 55), the individual white lines that define the bird's shattered plumage have a certain resemblance to the strong and purposeful thinning and thickening of strokes in Oriental painting, but they are fundamentally nonstructural and constitute no more than a surface pattern emphasized by their saliency against a dark background. Actually, the subject and mood are even further removed from the Oriental point of view. And this picture, like so many by this artist, is given an air of mystery by its tenebrous atmosphere. The theme, unquestionably handled with great sensitivity, presents a wounded, dying creature sinking into primordial blackness. Thus unnoticed these little things go to their death, as nature ever bears all her sons away. This very emphasis on dissolution and death is entirely non-Oriental. Death in the East is an accepted inevitable thing that comes to all men, and is without interest as a subject for morbid introspection or artistic inspiration in a tradition that has rather been concerned with the vitalization of whatever theme the artist chose. In art this is simply the reflection of fundamentally different attitudes in the philosophical and psychological make-up of East and West.

An ink painting of geese (figure 56) by the thirteenth-century painter, Mu-ch'i may be taken as an example of the kind of Oriental prototype that Graves may have had in mind. This picture is executed with great immediacy in the fewest possible strokes. The sure progression of the touch of the brush can be followed in its unerring placing on the paper. Just as each stroke is completely satisfying in itself, so the combination of all the strokes together give a perfect suggestion of the structure of the bird, its texture, and, above all, the quality of animation and movement that characterizes its flight. The relationship to space is abstractly implied by the blank paper surrounding the form. In a Chinese painting of this type the combination of brushstrokes is more than a decorative surface pattern. Beyond its intrinsic aesthetic appeal in terms of the subtle variegations in the value of the ink tones, it confers both form and texture on the object portrayed. All the elements of this technique are directed toward capturing the essence of the vitality and energy of the bird in flight, so that it becomes more than just a design of a flying goose, a kind of universal ideograph of flight itself. It is this combination of form, texture, and the vitalization of the subject within the limited monochrome technique that makes the work of Graves appear as no more than a decorative and self-conscious improvisation in the Oriental technique. The differences in mood and interpretation of a theme from nature are, as we have seen, to be explained by the differences in time and environment separating the two performances.

8. *The World of Flowers*

Except for occasional decorative panels in Roman wall-paintings and mosaics, the painting of flowers in the West has until comparatively modern times been subsidiary to one of the major categories of expres-

55. *Wounded Gull*

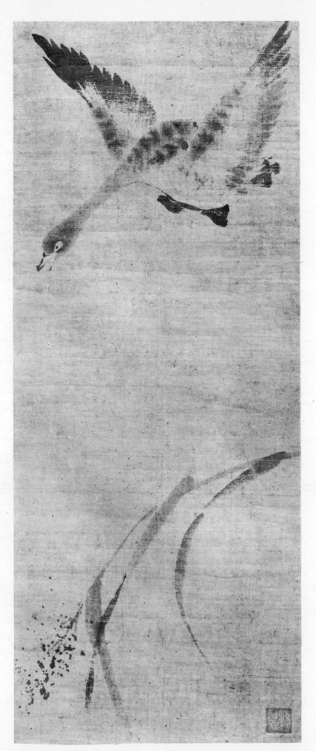

56. *Wild Goose*

sion: portraiture, religious painting, and landscape. Even there, before
the Renaissance, the individual flowers or groups of blossoms represented, fulfilled either a purely decorative or symbolic function. Certain flowers, like the rose and the lily, were appropriate emblems of
the Madonna, just as in the period before the beginning of a properly
speaking humanistic or scientific interest in nature, trees or branches
and leaves were only vaguely defined as symbolic references to a biblical figure. Flowers in art through the late medieval period were represented in a generalized decorative fashion, so that it is only in occasional capitals of the twelfth and thirteenth centuries that we begin to
discern a differentiation in species and some regard for the articulation
of the plant form. In the Renaissance of the fifteenth century, with
Western man's aroused interest in every facet of nature as a part of
the cosmos centering around him, flowers came to be painted not only
as references to sacred allegory but for their own intrinsic beauty of
growth, color, and texture. We are all familiar with the studies of
Leonardo and Dürer which have all the authority of botanical scientific recordings. There is a difference, however, between a scientific
drawing concerned with the exact limning of the outer skin of reality,
and the suggestion in naturalistic terms of the real inner nature of flowers, what we think of as their character and growth.

Probably no artist in the Renaissance revealed a greater sensitivity to
flowers and the sensuous beauty of their life than Sandro Botticelli
(1444–1510). His flowers differ in every way from the more formal
and patternized presentations of plant forms by earlier artists. Botticelli's
flowers were perhaps not scientifically perfect; one feels that they were
more loved than studied by an artist who saw these transient, beautiful
things as symbols of the sensuous life of all nature, as a revelation of
the organic sympathy of growth and change that unites all things in
nature's world. This is a quality that we can discern in the artist's drawing of flowers as animated nervous forms organized in exactly the
same restless and rhythmic lines that bestow such a spiritual vitality
to the same artist's representation of figures. Of course in many of Botticelli's paintings the flowers still retain their old iconographical ap-
propriateness for representations of the Madonna. And in his famous
panel of the "Primavera" the blossoms are selected as specific emblems
of spring (figure 57). Over and beyond this, they have a suggestion
of the freshness and fragility of daisies and lilies, such as has seldom
been achieved in Western art. The artist's awareness of the outward
sensuous beauties of nature, combined with a knowledge of structure,
was possible only in the Renaissance when observation replaced the
acceptance of all nature as an allegorical reference to the divine, when

58. *Lotus and Herons*

57. *Primavera (detail)*

in the neo-Platonic sense the beauty of God could be discerned in the contemplation of earthly loveliness.

Flower painting in the Far East has a very long history. Flowers were decoratively or symbolically represented as early as Han times (206 B.C.–220 A.D.). There are historical references to masters of this genre even in T'ang times and what are presumably copies of later periods give us an idea of the performance of the great artists of the tenth century when flower painting reached its classic perfection. A comparison for Botticelli's lyrical interpretation of flowers may be found in a famous panel of lotus blossoms belonging to Chion-in, Kyōto (figure 58). Traditionally this painting is attributed to Hsü Hsi (tenth century), but it may be a replica of the Sung period. Although this flower painting might strike us as realistic, there is an arbitrary distortion of natural space that tends to confer a pattern-like quality on the shapes silhouetted against the background. Here, as in so many Chinese paintings, there is no distinction between the space of foreground and background, so that without any idea of recession the shapes are, so to speak, forced outward to the picture plane, almost like cut-outs pinned to a screen. This is not to imply that the plants are like static designs or patterns in a rug. We are very definitely made aware of their movement as the wind moves through them, bending and rattling the fronds and tearing the petals from the fading blossoms. Just as Botticelli's daisies are a specific symbol of spring's reawakening, Far Eastern flower paintings always contain some poetic illusion; the panel attributed to Hsü Hsi is a kind of allegory of autumn with the idea of seasonal change and the transience of all nature conveyed in the little detail of the lotus flowers disintegrating in the chilling wind. One could say that here as in Botticelli there is an extraordinary feeling for the growth and sensuous beauty of the subject, conveyed in the appropriately pliant lines of the bending stems, in the delicate powdered suggestion of the fragile texture of the rose-tinted blossoms. Technically, the kinship extends to the Eastern and Western artists' employment of a kind of arbitrary shading with the greatest brilliance of color in shadow, a device which, although it provides only an abstract illusion of relief, makes for a sensuous coloristic richness, and appropriately connotes the indefinable iridescence of the flowers' butterfly texture.

Botticelli, through his sensuous awareness to the beauty of growing things as a reflection of the life of all things in nature, and Hsü Hsi, by his suggestion of the spirit rather than the outward form of reality, have given us the very essence of the world of flowers and its order.

Chapter Four

Still Life

STILL-LIFE paintings, more than any other mode of expression, are "artists' pictures": in this form the artist as nowhere else is able to experiment and work out for himself problems of composition, texture, color, and so on. All idea of content is usually absent, and the objects of inanimate nature are arranged according to some preconceived scheme of abstract harmony of shape, color, and mass. The painter can experiment to his heart's content with the solution of how to represent objects in space, how to achieve subtleties of balance through the arrangement of shapes and colors. For these reasons still-life paintings can be very personal; some may even be "self-portraits" of the artists through the associations evoked by the object in a particular arrangement.

The history of still-life painting in the ancient world extends, as every student knows, to the famous story of Zeuxis and Apelles and their paintings that deceived the birds and even human beholders. This was apparently a tradition of magic realism, in which the aim of the painter was to depict natural objects with such convincing verisimilitude as to deceive the spectator into thinking them real. There are further accounts of lost paintings of this type in the Hellenistic period. Copies of some of these lost originals exist in mosaic. It was from conquered Greece that the fashion for what today would be called *nature morte* spread to Rome.

A general account of the later history of still life in the Western tradition would have to include its revival as a specially appropriate theme for scientific recording of a microcosm of reality in the Renaissance, and its exploitation as a subject for experiments in light and texture from Baroque times to the nineteenth century. Modern art has seen a revival of still life in the artist's adventure into the realm of the abstract.

As will be explained in detail in the first section of this chapter, still-life painting in India exists only as a decorative adjunct to monumental decoration, with the possibility that these reproductions of fruits and flowers were intended as paintings of tangible offerings to the Buddha.

The subject matter of Oriental still-life painting can be grouped around a certain number of themes that are used over and over again by different artists, just as poets rework motifs such as love, death, spring and autumn, the wildflower, and others. In China these themes, like the isolated representation of flowering branches or fruit, have an underlying reference, recognizable to all, to the season of which they are typical. One will never find the dead birds and beasts that litter the groaning boards beloved of the seventeenth-century Dutch.

Still-life painting in the Far East cannot properly be described by the Western term, *nature morte*, with its implication of a collection of objects dead or inanimate, since such arrangements in Chinese and Japanese painting are in a sense as much alive as the most lifelike figure subject, with the same suggestion of growth and articulation.

1. *Wall Paintings*

The fragments of mosaics and wall paintings of still-life subjects that have been found in Roman cities could be described as dining-room pieces, since they served the same function of providing an interesting decoration for the triclinium as did the fruit-and-flower pieces in European and American dining-rooms as late as a generation ago. A typical example is the still life in Naples, representing a glass jar and fruits (figure 59). There is an Oriental comparison for this type of subject matter in the panels of fruit-and-flower subjects in the wall paintings at Ajanṭā. These latter paintings are details in the decoration of the

60. *Ceiling Decoration of Cave Temple*

59. *Still Life*

ceiling of Cave I, and were presumably executed in the sixth or early seventh century A.D. Although the examples chosen are similar in many respects, they reveal certain fundamental differences of approach and handling that continue to characterize treatment of this type of subject matter in European and Oriental art of all periods.

In examining the group at Naples we find the glass vessel and fruit displayed for us as though on open shelves. The jar and each separate piece of fruit is independently painted with the most meticulous attention to its texture, reflections, modeling, and even cast shadows; and yet there is not the slightest suggestion of the relationship of this collection of objects to one another. Even their position in space remains ambiguous, and there is no principle of design beyond the arrangement of these parts of the composition in parallel rows. One gets the impression from this and other surviving reflections of classical still life that the artists strove for an effect of *trompe-l'oeil* by their concentrated attention on the limning of individual details intensely observed and with little or no sense of an illusionistic spatial or atmospheric representation. The technique could be described as the *mode of relief*, in which the individual objects are given the illusion of roundness and solidity by carefully graduated shading within the local tone of a particular area, so that the shaded portions of the peaches are in a more neutralized tone of the same yellow-orange that is used for the areas in light. Neither in this nor in other examples of Roman still life of fruits or flowers is there the least suggestion of the life peculiar to these growing things. They are always completely inanimate and devoid of any arrangement in terms of compositional pattern.

For Indian still life we can find a great many examples in the individual panels of fruits and flowers that surround the main figural compositions on the ceiling of Cave I at Ajaṇṭā (figure 60). Some of these compositions contain objects like conch shells that may have an allegorical reference to Buddhism, but for the most part they may be described as representations of the kind of offerings of fruits and flowers that would be acceptable on the altars of Buddha. At the same time they are elements of a magnificent decorative scheme.

The technique of painting the floral details at Ajaṇṭā is the same that is employed for the great figural compositions of the walls. It consists of outline and local tone reinforced with a kind of abstract shading. In this chiaroscuro we have a graduation in value of the hue of a green leaf or orange flower, so that an illusion of modeling or relief is produced. This method of modeling from full intensity to white is, of course, the same mode of relief employed by medieval and early Renais-

sance painters in Europe. Such allusions as there are to painting in early
Indian literature invariably contain a reference to the effect of *trompe-
l'oeil* produced by the painter's ability to suggest the illusion of relief
on a flat surface. The individual decorative panels at Ajaṇṭā are so filled
with floral and vegetable forms that they give the effect of a bursting
luxuriance. In spite of this profusion of details we never have the sense
of the completely separate, unrelated existence of these elements, as
we do in the Herculaneum fresco. These parts are always related to an
integrated design that spreads to the edges of the frame in rhythmic,
curvilinear motifs. The result is not only a singularly moving pattern,
but the repetition in the sinuous curving lines of stems, leaves, and
petals gives an extraordinary suggestion of actual growth and vitality
to these natural forms. There is never any suggestion of texture beyond
what is implied by differentiations in color, and the abstract character
of the modeling gives the illusion that we are looking at a painted relief rather than a realistic representation of still life.

Although there is a certain resemblance between the Indian and
Roman still life in the painters' suggestion of an illusion of reality in
terms of relief modeling, and even if there is an ultimate derivation
from the West for this technique in India, the comparison is one which,
in actuality, illustrates the fundamental difference between the Western and Indian points of view. There is something not only European
but specifically Latin in the Roman painter's concern for material reality and its objective recording in the completely cold and separate portrayal of the individual objects comprising the arrangement, with interest neither in their animation nor organization in terms of moving
design. In looking at the panels at Ajaṇṭā, one has the feeling that the
painter's suggestion of tangible form in terms of relief is only a sub-
ordinate part of the whole conception and not in any sense scientific
in intent. The artist's primary aim appears to have been the imparting
of a sense of vitality, a kind of stirring, blowing movement, with which
the plant forms are imbued through the artist's dynamic organization
of the pattern of linear motifs that are the basis of his design. It is this
suggestion of breathing aliveness, combined with a cadenced rhythm of
pattern, that can be found in every category of Indian art, in the representation of human figures, animals, and all growing things. Even in
still life we can recognize the principle of Indian painting, whereby the
painter is bound to invest his creations with the breath of life, and that
other injunction of the painter's manual, where it is stated that every
artist must be acquainted with the rhythmic language of movement
found in the Indian dance.

2. *Matisse and a Ming Master*

Just as modern painters in the West have indulged in a deliberate distortion of reality, because realism for them was associated with the academic tradition, so in Ming China some of the gentlemen-painters like Shên Chou (1427–1509) indulged in a kind of whimsical avoidance of those realistic effects of drawing and painting that for them were associated with the work of the merely professional painters. In some of his ink plays Shên Chou gives us the same kind of negation of reality that we think modern in Henri Matisse (1869–   ). Typical of this point of view is a picture dated in 1502, a still life of an orange, a chrysanthemum, and a water bottle (figure 62). This picture is no more than a fugitive improvisation in which we may imagine the artist was rather pleased with his deliberately bad drawing that flattens out the shapes to patterns defined in terms of the surest ink line, a line that itself arrests the eye, as does the moving contour of the Matisse drawing (figure 61). This sort of thing by Shên Chou might be compared with the laconic statements of the Ch'an Buddhist artists of the Sung period, who in a few lightninglike bolts and strokes created the final essence of objects in ink. This was a technique developed by the Ch'an artist to record with immediacy the instantaneous impression of a fleeting vision. Shên Chou could be described as a more modern artist and a more self-conscious one in his deliberate distortion for aesthetic effect and his realization of the independent aesthetic attraction of the slight ink and brush texture in itself. As one of his Chinese critics said, "The freer and easier, the truer were his paintings. The simpler he was, the further he reached."

There are a great many still-life drawings, like the one reproduced, from every period of Matisse's career (figure 61) that bear a superficial resemblance to Shên Chou's picture in their deliberate simplification and ingenuous freshness. One could say that this artist was concerned at once with the essential and aesthetic qualities of subjects, their purely formal relationships, and what might be called their personalities. Although the wit and drama of Matisse's distortions may be less conscious than they were in Shên Chou, he is interested in the emotions and associations they evoke in terms of shape and color. The aesthetic problems that have confronted Matisse as a modern artist certainly did not concern Shên Chou. For Matisse the still life has always been a struggle for the resolution of the problem of subtleties of balance, between decoration and reality, the active and static character of his forms, and the contrast of patterns and surfaces simple and complex. Matisse's experi-

62. *Still Life*

61. *Flowers*

ments in the contrast of plain and ornamented surfaces, his juxtaposition of colors of high, jewel-like intensity, and his reduction of reality to pattern shapes drily inscribed in black contours, would have been totally unintelligible to the great artist of fifteenth-century China. The drawing of figure 61 is a complete statement of Matisse's formula in black and white. Matisse's often brilliant essays in the solution of what are really abstract problems in the balance of both form and color belong entirely to the Western world of the postimpressionist period. The resemblance to Shên Chou rests entirely on the similarity of their reduction of objects to flat, decorative shapes in what is a sort of succinct and witty characterization of their essential forms.

FOR FURTHER READING

According to the Introduction, this book is not intended as a survey either in a historical or typological way. Its usefulness resides in introducing the Western reader to a different approach in looking at the masterpieces of his own tradition in their relation to the art of the Oriental world. The selections offered for analysis are only typical examples of this approach and they represent but a small sample of the opportunity for comparisons that this method affords; for example, no attempt has been made here to include architecture, but it is obvious that many types of buildings, such as Christian basilicas and Buddhist chaitya-halls, Gothic cathedrals and Hindu temples, offer possible, similar comparisons on the basis of their resemblances in spiritual and stylistic expression.

The choice of the works of art discussed in this book has been conditioned by the availability of examples in the various categories of works of art which, by their basic resemblance in subject, style, and mood, provide a point of departure for a useful comparison of Western and Oriental aims and techniques. It has perhaps offended some readers that many of the great names in the history of European art—Raphael, Rubens, Rembrandt, Velasquez, and others—have been unjustly omitted. In reply to this criticism it should be restated here, as suggested in the Introduction, that the masters of the post-Renaissance period both in their preoccupation with the solution of the problem of total visual effect and the nature of their technique in terms of heavy impasto are so completely opposite to the Oriental artist's approach and method that the work of these European masters does not afford a basis for mutual comparison. In exactly the same way, although occasional superficial resemblances in the mood or even the subject matter of modern art provide useful contrasts with Asiatic painting, we can find no counterparts in the Orient for the nonobjective movement with its total negation not only of content but of the very probity of the craft.

Many readers for whom this book has been an introduction to both Western and Eastern art may wish to explore further the pathways indicated herein. Although there are no books that specifically follow the present scheme of analysis, the monumental work, *The Voices of Silence* by André Malraux (New York: Doubleday, Garden City, 1953) provides occasional comparisons of the art of Orient and Occident. Georges Duthuit's *Chinese Mysticism and Modern Painting* (Paris: Chroniques du jour, 1936) is a collection of works of art that do have an accidental and superficial similarity never satisfactorily explained or justified in the flowery text that accompanies them.

This is perhaps the place to recommend other accounts of separate categories of art considered in this book. Certainly the finest treatment of landscape is Kenneth Clark's *Landscape Painting* (New York: Scribner, 1950).

Max Friedlander's *Landscape, Portrait, Still-life* (New York: Philosophical Library, 1950) includes stimulating chapters on the characteristics of these modes of expression in Western art. Another useful general work that analyzes examples of these categories, as well as the development of the religious subject matter in art is Paul Zucker's *Styles in Painting* (New York: Viking Press, 1950). A fascinating and indispensable treatment of official portraiture in the West is Marianna Jenkins' *The State Portrait* (College Art Association, Study No. 3, 1947). Sacheverell Sitwell's introduction to the Faber booklet on Audubon's birds provides a detailed account of this branch of nature painting.

For those who wish a complete chronological treatment of Western art, I can recommend D. M. Robb and J. J. Garrison, *Art in the Western World* (New York: Harper and Brothers, 1942) and E. Gombrich, *The Story of Art* (New York: Phaidon, 1952). A few specialized books that provide a further analysis of the types of art included in this work may be suggested here: E. Cecchi, *The Sienese Painters of the Trecento* (London and New York: F. Warne & Co., 1931); G. Richter, *Sculpture and Sculptors of the Greeks* (New Haven: Yale University Press, 1929); D. Talbot Rice, *Byzantine Art* (Oxford: Clarendon Press, 1935).

No one satisfactory history of all Oriental art exists, although a number of separate treatments of art in different regions of the East can be suggested. An extensive bibliography of all phases of Far Eastern art will be found in my *Harvard Outline and Reading Lists for Oriental Art* (Cambridge: Harvard University Press, 1952). Although it would be impractical to list all of the books in which subjects discussed in this book are mentioned, the following may prove useful to readers who wish further accounts of these works in their historical relationship: Benjamin Rowland, *The Art and Architecture of India* (Baltimore: Penguin Books, 1953); O. Sirén, *History of Early Chinese Painting* (London: Medici Society, 1933), and *History of Later Chinese Painting* (London: Medici Society, 1938); H. Minamoto and H. G. Henderson, *An Illustrated History of Japanese Art* (Kyōto: Hoshino, 1935); L. Warner, *The Enduring Art of Japan* (Cambridge: Harvard University Press, 1952); W. Cohn, *Chinese Painting* (London: Phaidon, 1948).

INDEX